THE Lewis & Clark EXPEDITION

Join the Corps of Discovery to Explore Uncharted Territory

Carol A. Johmann

Illustrations by
Michael Kline

WILLIAMSON PUBLISHING • CHARLOTTE, VT

Library of Congress Cataloging-in-Publication Data

Johmann, Carol A., 1949–
    The Lewis & Clark Expedition : join the Corps of Discovery to explore uncharted territory / Carol A. Johmann ; illustrations by Michael Kline.
        p. cm.
    "A Kaleidoscope Kids book."
    Includes index.
    Summary: Describes the expedition led by Lewis and Clark to explore the unknown western regions of America at the beginning of the nineteenth century. Includes related activities.
    ISBN 1-885593-73-2 (pbk.)
    1. Lewis and Clark Expedition (1804-1806)--Juvenile literature. 2. West (U.S.)--Discovery and exploration--Juvenile literature. 3. West (U.S.)--Description and travel--Juvenile literature. 4. West (U.S.)--Discovery and exploration--Study and teaching--Activity programs--Juvenile literature. [1. Lewis and Clark Expedition (1804-1806) 2. West (U.S.)--Discovery and exploration.] I. Title: Lewis and Clark Expedition. II. Kline, Michael, P., ill. III. Title.

F592.7 .J63 2003
917.804'2--dc21

                                                      2003028075

Kaleidoscope Kids® series editor: **Susan Williamson**
Project editor: **Vicky Congdon**
Interior design: **Dana Pierson**
Interior illustrations: **Michael Kline**
Cover design: **Black Fish Design**
Cover illustrations: **Michael Kline**
Printing: **Quebecor World**

Printed in Canada

Williamson Publishing Co.
P. O. Box 185
Charlotte, Vermont 05445
1-800-234-8791

10 9 8 7 6 5 4 3 2 1

Kids Can!®, Little Hands®, Kaleidoscope Kids®, Quick Starts for Kids!®, and Tales Alive!® are registered trademarks of Williamson Publishing.

Good Times™ and You Can Do It!™ are trademarks of Williamson Publishing.

Notice: The information contained in this book is true, complete, and accurate to the best of our knowledge. All recommendations and suggestions are made without any guarantees on the part of the author or Williamson Publishing. The author and publisher disclaim all liability incurred in connection with the use of this information.

Dedication

To my "big" sister Nancy, who accepted me as her almost "equal partner" as we explored the dunes, beaches, and woods around our grandparents' home many summers ago.

For more Williamson Publishing books by Carol Johmann, please see page 112.

Acknowledgments

Many thanks to everyone at Williamson Publishing and to Michael Kline for all their efforts in turning my manuscript into a book. For the quotations, I used Gary E. Moulton's and Donald Jackson's editions of the journals. For complete acknowledgments, see page 108.

Photography/Illustration: page 16: Clark's sketch of the keelboat, Yale Collection of Western Americana, Beinecke Rare Book and Manuscript Library; page 22: reproduction keelboat, © Mike Whye, Council Bluffs, IA; page 24: portrait of Meriwether Lewis, Independence National Historical Park, Philadelphia, PA; page 25: portrait of William Clark, Denver Public Library, Western History Collection, call #Z-244; page 37: blunderbuss, Robert Miller, LionGate Arms & Armour, Scottsdale, AZ; page 49: Captains Lewis and Clark hold a council with Indians, Gass, Patrick. A *Journal of the Voyages and Travels of a Corps of Discovery,* Philadelphia, 1812. pg. 30, Rare Books Division, The New York Public Library, Astor, Lenox and Tilden Foundations; page 53: *Mih-Tutta-Hangkusch, A Mandan Village,* Joslyn Art Museum, Omaha, NE, Gift of Enron Art Foundation; page 70: *Lewis's First Glimpse of the Rockies,* painting by Olaf Seltzer, registration #0137.756, From the Collection of Gilcrease Museum, Tulsa, OK; page 71: Heath Cock or Cock of the Plains [also known as Sage Grouse], Entry of 2 March 1806, Clarks Papers, Missouri Historical Society Archives, St. Louis, MO; page 83: Lewis's woodpecker, courtesy of the American Philosophical Society, Philadelphia, PA; page 85: Clark's journal entry, courtesy of the American Philosophical Society, Philadelphia, PA; page 89: knob-top hat, Peabody Museum, Harvard University, Photo N31728; page 95: portrait of *Mehkeme-Sukah, Blackfoot Chief,* Joslyn Art Museum, Omaha, NE, Gift of Enron Art Foundation; pages 47, 50, 72, and 88: courtesy of the National Park Service, Jefferson National Expansion Memorial, St. Louis, MO; cover art (background) and pages 51, 52, and 104: PicturesNow.com, San Rafael, CA.

CONTENTS

JEFFERSON'S DREAM

Thomas Jefferson, the third president of the United States, could do anything, it sometimes seemed. He designed Monticello, his plantation home in Charlottesville, Virginia. As a naturalist, he kept records of rainfall and temperature, described the migration of birds, and noted the dates when flowers bloomed. He conducted the country's first archaeological survey. He invented a curved plow and predicted that carriages would someday be powered by steam engines.

Most of all, Jefferson was a big thinker. In the Declaration of Independence, he wrote that "all men are created equal" and that people have the right to "Life, Liberty and the pursuit of Happiness." He believed the federal government should stay small and interfere as little as possible in people's lives. What big thoughts did Jefferson have as he took the presidential oath on March 4, 1801? On that day he asked Americans "to unite with one heart and one mind." He was talking about bringing political parties together, but it's likely he was also referring to expanding the nation westward.

Westward expansion, Jefferson believed, would make the country safer from foreign invasion. It would secure trading rights along the Mississippi River for American settlers, and it would give the nation room to grow for generations to come. If Americans explored the West, they could take a claim to it. Jefferson and others had tried to arrange that several times before. Now, as president, he'd be able to send an expedition — and he had already hired as his secretary the man who would lead it.

The West: Who Claimed What

* CLAIMED BY BRITAIN AND THE UNITED STATES.

* * * OREGON COUNTRY CLAIMED BY BRITAIN, RUSSIA, SPAIN, AND THE UNITED STATES.

British Canada

Oregon Country

Columbia River

Snake River

* * *

Louisiana (France)

Missouri

Spanish Territory

Indiana Territory (U.S.)

Mississippi

Ohio River

United States

Rio Grande

* *

New Orleans

Spanish Florida

* * LAND BETWEEN THE SOUTHERN BORDER OF THE LOUISIANA PURCHASE AND THE RIO GRANDE CLAIMED BY SPAIN AND THE UNITED STATES.

However the West shaped up, many nations besides the United States wanted it. In 1801, Spain claimed Florida, Texas, the Southwest, and California. It had just given the middle of the continent, Louisiana (at that time, a much larger area than the present-day state), back to France. Between them, France and Spain controlled the trading rights along the Mississippi River and the important port of New Orleans.

South of the Great Lakes, Britain still had forts and trading posts. British trappers dominated trade with the Indians there, exchanging goods and guns for furs. The Russians also sought furs. Seventeen years earlier they had crossed the *Bering Strait* (the narrow waterway between North America and Asia) and set up the first non-native settlement in Alaska. Now they were considering a move down the coast.

The Main Goal: Finding the Northwest Passage

Why all the interest in the West? People assumed it had lots of natural resources, like animals for furs, gold, and silver. They also assumed it had rivers — the key to moving resources and goods (important products like guns, cloth, tea) across the continent. If one western river flowed into another, you wouldn't need to sail around the tip of South America — a risky trip that could take three years! — to trade with China and India.

For centuries, explorers had searched in vain for a Northwest Passage — an all-water route across North America. Jefferson believed that one existed from the Mississippi to the Pacific Ocean, and he made finding a water route suitable for trade the main goal of the Lewis and Clark expedition.

It was known that the Missouri River flowed into the Mississippi (see map, page 5). From sea explorations in the late 1700s, it was also known that the Columbia River emptied into the Pacific. Trader Jean Baptiste Truteau (true-TOE) had reported in 1796 that he'd been told by an American Indian that the Missouri River originated in "great mountains of rock" beyond which another "wide and deep river" flowed "in the direction of the winter sunset" to "a large body of water, the other bank of which was not visible."

If, Jefferson surmised, both the Missouri and the Columbia had sources near each other in the western mountains, and if those mountains were rounded and pretty easy to cross like the Appalachians, those rivers might form a Northwest Passage.

Meet Secretary Lewis

To explore the West, Jefferson wanted someone who knew about river travel, the wilderness, and Indian culture. Who better than a young friend named Meriwether Lewis, who was 26, unmarried, and had served as a captain in the U.S. Army on the frontier? Like Jefferson, he was a dreamer and a thinker. He was strong, brave, and curious. He understood the Army, knew the wilderness, and was familiar with Indian culture. He was also intelligent. Whatever Lewis didn't know, Jefferson figured, he and others could teach him.

For Lewis, being secretary to Jefferson was a marvelous time. Copying reports and letters might be boring, but his other duties were exciting. He carried President Jefferson's messages around Washington, D.C. Jefferson hated public speaking, so Lewis delivered the State of the Union address outlining the nation's issues and new policies in front of Congress. He spent evenings with Jefferson, entertaining famous people. Best of all, Lewis got to read Jefferson's books and listen to him talk about geography, science, politics, and Indian affairs, while they ate meals together and took walks along the Potomac River. It was the beginning of Lewis's training for the expedition.

Time to Start Planning

Only Jefferson and Lewis lived at the White House. It was so quiet at first that Jefferson wrote they were "like two mice in a church." The quiet ended in the summer of 1802 with, of all things, a book! A Scottish-born Canadian fur trader named Alexander Mackenzie had explored western Canada, and in 1793, he reached the Pacific Ocean north of what is now Vancouver. His route was mostly over land and not practical for trade, but in 1801, he published a book urging Britain to set up forts and trading posts in the West.

That worried Jefferson. He realized Americans had to act right away if they wanted to beat the British. He and Lewis began planning an expedition to start the next year. They talked about its size (not so big it would frighten the Indians) and the route (up the Missouri, across the mountains, then down the Columbia). They discussed the importance of mapping the region, observing new wildlife and plants, and keeping records. And they decided that, unlike Mackenzie's trip, it would be as much a scientific expedition and an opportunity to increase trade as an exploration of unknown territory.

Will Congress Approve?

On January 18, 1803, Jefferson wrote to Congress that "an intelligent officer with ten or twelve chosen men" from the Army could explore the "whole line" of the Missouri River, "even to the western Ocean." Along the way, the officer could talk with the different Indian nations about sites for trading posts. The expedition would need guns, some instruments, and "cheap presents" for the Indians. It would cost an estimated $2,500 plus the gifts of land the soldiers would get when they returned. Would Congress approve? Yes!

The Louisiana Purchase

"Let the Land rejoice, for you have bought Louisiana for a Song."

—*General Horatio Gates to President Thomas Jefferson, July 18, 1803*

Under Napoleon Bonaparte, France had been fighting wars around the world, trying to build an empire. Now that France had control of Louisiana (see map, page 5), Jefferson worried that Napoleon (he's often referred to by his first name) would close New Orleans and the Mississippi River to American trade. The president warned him that if France landed troops in Louisiana, the United States would fight. The country might even join with its old enemy Britain against its former ally France. Napoleon didn't like that idea. He had been at war with Britain on and off for years.

Trying to deal with things peacefully, Jefferson got permission from Congress to offer to buy New Orleans. He sent his trusted friend James Monroe to Paris to bargain with the French. A former senator from Virginia, Monroe had also been a minister to France (in this sense, a *minister* is a government official). What a surprise it must have been when the French foreign minister asked, "How much will you give for the whole of Louisiana?" Although Monroe had permission to spend only $9 million, he agreed to pay $15 million for the whole territory. Just like that, the United States bought half of the West!

A Picture Is Worth a Thousand Words

To a lot of folks, looking at maps isn't the exciting part of history. They'd rather get involved in the action, the strategies, and the personalities of the participants. We can understand that, as we each have our personal preferences. But we hope you will look at the maps in this book when you see cross-references to them.

You see, maps really are pictures worth thousands of words. They tell the story of relationships between countries and people, of plans that don't work out, and of unexpected challenges. If you think of a person trying to get from here to there, and you look at a map, well, you can clearly see why something happened the way it did. Maps tell it like it is.

Happy Birthday, America!

Although the treaty to purchase Louisiana was signed on April 30, 1803, it took a long time for the news to reach the United States. American newspapers announced the purchase on the Fourth of July, on the country's 27th birthday. The purchase was so popular hardly anyone minded that it cost more money than Congress had approved — or that it was more money than the nation had in its treasury! Who cared about money when their country just doubled in size! And who could argue it wasn't the best land deal ever at 828,000 square miles (2,144,500 sq km) for just three cents an acre (0.4 hectare).

Well, some spoilsports *did* care, pointing out it was a wasteland. And what about Jefferson's belief that the federal government should stay small? And could the United States stay united if it became so much bigger?

TRY IT!

Eventually the Louisiana Territory gave rise to 13 new states. Check the map on page 5 where their outlines are marked. Can you name them? Check your answer against the list of states below, and if you need to, check a map to locate them.

Why Did Napoleon Sell?

Building empires costs money, whether you buy one the way Jefferson did or go to war as Napoleon did. France had just lost a lot of money, along with most of its troops, while fighting a slave revolt in Haiti, a French colony in the Caribbean Sea. That loss taught Napoleon that France probably couldn't defend Louisiana so he decided that he might as well sell the land and get the money. One aspect of the arrangement particularly delighted Napoleon: A larger United States would begin to pose a threat to Britain. "I have given England a rival," he declared, "who, sooner or later, will humble her pride." Yes, Napoleon certainly didn't like England!

NAPOLEON BONAPARTE

Try it! answer: Louisiana (first to be admitted to the United States in 1812), Missouri (1821), Arkansas (1836), Iowa (1846), Minnesota (1858), Kansas (1861), Nebraska (1867), Colorado (1876), North Dakota (1889), South Dakota (1889), Montana (1889), Wyoming (1890), and Oklahoma (1907).

Do You Agree?

Historians consider the Louisiana Purchase to have had a bigger impact on the development of the United States than any other event in U.S. history except those things that made the country possible — the Declaration of Independence, the American Revolution, and the Constitution. The Louisiana Purchase:

- opened the Mississippi River for trade

- removed a foreign power, France, from the continent

- provided vast amounts of fertile land for farming

- supplied resources like oil, gold, and silver

- doubled the size of the nation

- offered land and opportunity for millions of immigrants from around the world who would pour into the country over the next century

But there was an enormous price to pay for all of this — and not in terms of dollars. The impact of the Louisiana Purchase was devastating to the American Indians in the West. Within just a few generations, the massive migration of white people into the West and the United States government's policy toward the Indians led to the end of their way of life as it had been for thousands of years before the U.S. was born.

Jefferson's Instructions

Even before the land purchase became official, Jefferson had begun to consult experts and politicians about the expedition. Aside from his main goal of finding a water route west, Jefferson had other important objectives, which he detailed in a long memo to Lewis:

- to plot the Missouri's tributaries, islands, and rapids using various instruments.

- to tell the American Indian nations along the way of the United States' "wish to be neighborly, friendly, and useful to them." Lewis was to note their names, estimate their populations, and learn about their languages and cultures. Why? One, because Jefferson was curious, and, two, because he thought it would be a good way to get the Indians to accept trade with the United States.

- to gather plant and animal specimens, keep weather records, take soil samples, and examine fossils and minerals. All observations, Jefferson wrote, were "to be taken with great pains & accuracy, to be entered distinctly and intelligibly" into journals.

Just two weeks after finishing the instructions, Jefferson learned of the Louisiana Purchase. His excitement grew. Now the expedition would be on American soil all the way to the Rockies! The captains would only have to worry about foreign countries west of the mountains.

THINK ABOUT IT

Who Owns the Earth?

The struggles between peoples all over the world seem to involve one of two things: borders (ownership of land) or religious freedom (and sometimes a confusing mix of the two). It happens over and over throughout the history of mankind. The Romans set the tone as they conquered more and more people to build the Roman Empire thousands of years ago. And this struggle is still being played out right now all over the world, in Ireland, the Middle East, and the African nations, just to name a few. How would you decide who "owns" or rules the land?

CRAMMING FOR THE TRIP

In the spring of 1803, Captain Meriwether Lewis was preparing to command one of the greatest explorations of all time. President Jefferson sent Lewis to Pennsylvania to study with experts so that he could plan, organize, and choose the right people to go along — all things that were essential for the expedition to succeed.

It was up to Lewis to decide how many men, what kinds of boats, how much food, and what medicines to take. Then he had to buy what he needed and organize it all. It was an enormous task, based in large part on unknowns, with life-threatening consequences resting on Lewis's choices and ultimate decisions.

Filling in the Map

Albert Gallatin, Jefferson's Secretary of the Treasury, had a special map of the West made for Lewis. There were only three places with known positions on it: St. Louis, the Mandan (MAN-dan) Indian villages on the upper Missouri, and the mouth of the Columbia River. To fill in the map, Lewis would have to measure latitude and longitude at places along the route.

Lewis learned to use a *sextant* to determine latitude and a special clock called a *chronometer* (kro-NOM-it-er) to calculate longitude. Unfortunately, the chronometer Lewis brought on the expedition stopped working, so he turned to a method that involved measuring the moon's movement in relation to certain stars. Calculating longitude from these measurements was so complicated, however, that he and Clark used estimates for their maps.

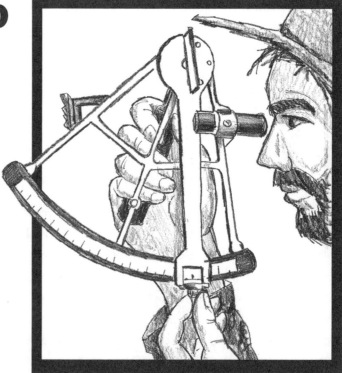

TO DETERMINE LATITUDE, LEWIS USED A SEXTANT TO MEASURE THE ANGLE BETWEEN THE SUN AND THE HORIZON AT NOON.

Say "Ahhhh"!

Dr. Benjamin Rush, the country's most famous physician at that time, believed two things could cure most ailments: *bleeding* (draining blood from a vein in a person's arm) and *purging* (making the sick person throw up or get diarrhea). He showed Lewis how to bleed and helped him put together a medicine kit with surgical instruments, herbs, and drugs. It included 50 dozen (that's 600!) of Rush's homemade pills, a strong *laxative* (a drug that helps to relieve constipation) nicknamed "Rush's Thunderbolts." (Apparently, bathroom humor was around in the 1800s, too!) Dr. Rush also recommended that the men wash their feet in cold water every morning (to make the men heartier) and wear flannel next to the skin to help stay dry in wet weather. Finally, Dr. Rush gave Lewis a long list of questions about the diseases and medical practices of Indians. He also wanted to know how they worshiped, punished murderers, and buried their dead.

Ask the Indians?

Why do you suppose an expert like Dr. Rush wanted to learn about disease from the Indians? It's interesting that he also wanted to know about worship, punishment, and burial, as these are all life-and-death rituals related to the very nature of being human. Do you think he respected the elders of the native tribes and hoped to learn from their wisdom and experience? Or do you think he was merely curious about the Indians' traditions?

Where the Wild Things Are

Dr. Caspar Wistar, another well-known physician at that time, urged Lewis to look out for some amazing critters, including woolly mammoths (many people believed these prehistoric creatures still existed in 1800!). But just in case they no longer existed, he showed Lewis how to look for their fossils in rocks and mud flats and how to collect their bones. Wistar was an expert on fossils and wrote the first American textbook on *anatomy* (the study of animals' skeletons and muscles). Yes, this expedition was about a lot more than tracing a cross-country route.

Collecting and Classifying

Jefferson and Lewis expected the expedition to come across living things that Americans and Europeans had never seen before, and they wanted to be sure these plants and animals would be carefully observed and accurately described.

For a scientific study, they knew you need to collect specimens very carefully, then *classify* (sort) and name them. On walks at Monticello and along the Potomac River, the president taught Lewis the biological classification system that scientists use to classify all living things. In Philadelphia, Dr. Benjamin Smith Barton showed Lewis how to gather seeds, preserve plant and animal *specimens* (samples), and label them with the date and place where they were found. Dr. Barton really knew this stuff — he was the first American to write a textbook on *botany*, the scientific study of plants. And Lewis took his assignment very, very seriously.

⊶ ⊱ TRY IT! ⊶ ⊱

Do you ever *notice* things without really *seeing* them, especially things that are very familiar to you? Well, that is exactly what Lewis was *not* supposed to do. He was to notice and then to *observe* very closely all things great and small.

Give it a try and see how you do. Go outside and pick up five leaves or blossoms from different plants, or look at different birds from your window. Look closely at shape, coloration, and size. Can you observe the details that make one different from another? Try sketching them. Now imagine carefully doing this day after day as you travel through hundreds of miles (km) of wilderness as Lewis did!

Shop 'til You Drop!

All during the spring of 1803, Lewis was buying supplies as well as studying. But he didn't know how many men would come on the expedition, or how long it would take, or what would be out there. With that many unknowns, it must have been a tough job to shop for the expedition. (And it wasn't as if he could stop at the corner store later on to pick up what he had forgotten!) So, what did he buy?

- camping equipment like tents, field tables with folding legs, kettles, mosquito netting, fishhooks, axes, knives, *flints* (stones that make a spark when struck with metal to start a fire), and candles

- personal supplies for the men like clothes, blankets, knapsacks, soap, tobacco, whiskey, needles, and thread

- food, including bushels of salt and spices, and 193 pounds (88 kg) of "portable soup," a dried soup of beans and vegetables

- weapons, including an *air gun* (uses compressed air to fire the bullet), rifles (for hunting), *muskets* (more powerful guns typically loaded from the open end), gunpowder for the muskets, and lead for making bullets

- gifts and trading goods for Indians, including peace medals, colored beads, scissors, brass thimbles, earrings, mirrors, calico shirts, red silk handkerchiefs, knives, tomahawks, and red body paint

- instruments for surveying and taking latitude and longitude readings, plus scales, compasses, and thermometers

- reference books on plants, animals, minerals, anatomy, and astronomy, in *oilskin* (a waterproofed cloth) bags to protect them

JEFFERSON PEACE MEDAL

Getting There

To transport his men and supplies up the Missouri, Lewis chose a keelboat and two pirogues (pea-ROGUES), one painted red, one white. A *keelboat* is a riverboat designed to carry a lot of weight. It has a *keel* — a heavy piece of wood that runs along the center of the bottom — to help control the boat in river currents. Lewis designed a large keelboat specifically for the expedition and ordered it to be constructed in Pittsburgh. Similar to canoes, the pirogues probably looked like flat-bottomed rowboats with masts. Both the keelboat and the pirogues could be rowed, sailed, pushed using long poles, or towed by ropes from the shore or shallow water.

Lewis also designed a collapsible canoe with an iron frame that could be covered with animal skins. He planned to use it later in the trip. Called *Experiment*, it weighed only 44 pounds (20 kg), but could carry one ton (.907 t) of weight.

IN HIS FIELD NOTES, WILLIAM CLARK SKETCHED THE KEELBOAT LEWIS DESIGNED.

IT WAS 55 FEET (16.5 M) LONG AND 8 FEET (2.4 M) WIDE AT THE MIDDLE. ITS MAST WAS 32 FEET (9.6 M) TALL AND HAD A JOINT AT ITS BASE SO IT COULD BE LOWERED WHEN THE WEATHER WASN'T GOOD FOR SAILING. THERE WAS A CABIN AT THE *STERN* (BACK) AND 11 BENCHES ACROSS THE DECK, EACH FOR TWO OARSMEN.

BUILD A KEELBOAT

Build a miniature replica of the keelboat Lewis and Clark took on the expedition! You can raise and lower the sail as well as the mast, position the mast's crosspiece, and even steer the boat with its movable rudder. This is a project where four hands are better than two, so invite a friend to help.

Supplies

- 2 pieces of airplane-model balsa wood, $\frac{3}{32}$" x 4" x 48" (2.4 mm x 10 cm x 122 cm), from a craft or hobby store
- Ruler
- Pencil
- Craft knife (or paring knife)*
- Cutting board
- Scissors
- Glue
- Masking tape
- Can, about 2" (5 cm) in diameter
- 1 balsa stick, $\frac{1}{4}$" x $\frac{1}{4}$" x 24" (5 mm x 5 mm x 60 cm)
- 2 small paper clips
- 1 balsa block, 1" x 1" x 3" (25 mm x 25 mm x 7.5 cm)
- 1 balsa stick, $\frac{1}{16}$" x $\frac{1}{4}$" x 24" (1.25 mm x 5 mm x 60 cm)
- White cloth, about 8" (20 cm) square
- 2 large paper clips
- Light string or thread

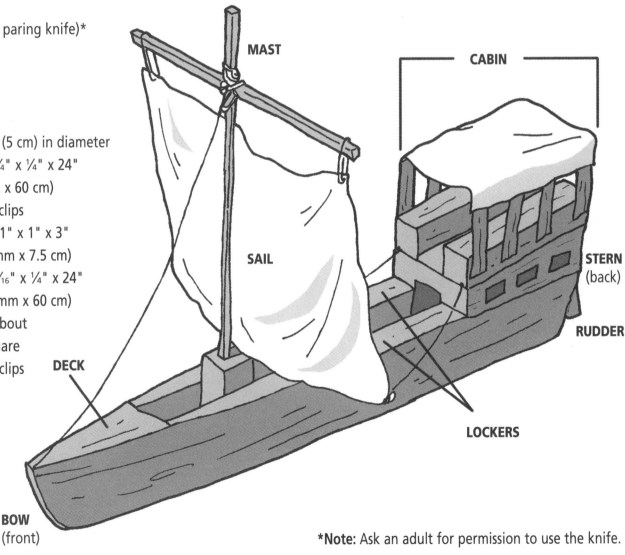

MAST

CABIN

SAIL

STERN (back)

RUDDER

DECK

LOCKERS

BOW (front)

*Note: Ask an adult for permission to use the knife.

To cut the wood:

Measure and mark the dimensions and label the sections on the two strips of balsa as shown. Carpenters say "measure twice, cut once," so double-check that your measurements are correct and your lines are straight. Using the ruler to guide the knife, cut the pieces out on the cutting board.

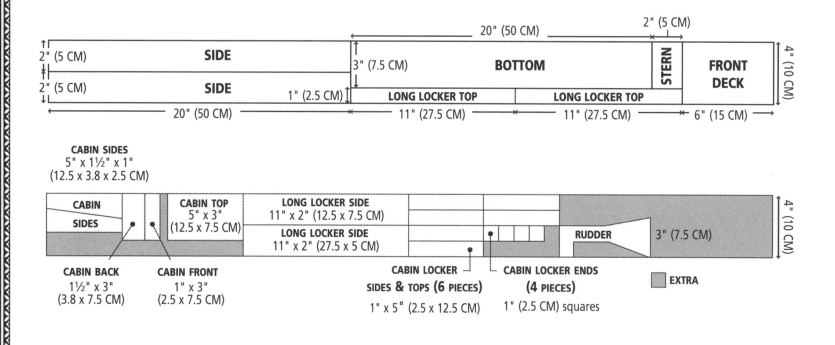

To build the boat:

❶ Mark one long SIDE piece as shown and cut it with scissors. Use it as a pattern for the other SIDE.

Glue the STERN piece to both side pieces (use tape to hold the pieces together while the glue dries).

❷ Place the BOTTOM piece on top of several long strips of tape, sticky side up.

Glue the stern and the back halves of the sides to the bottom piece, then bring the tape up both sides.

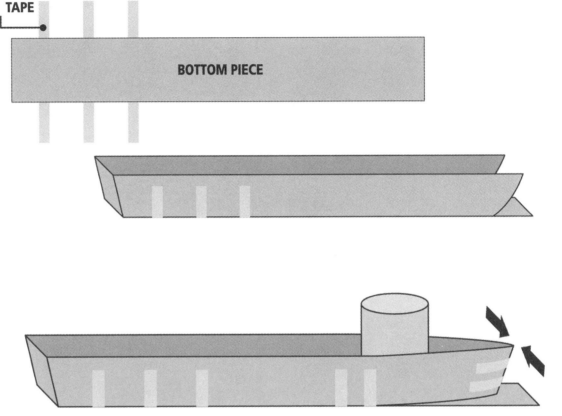

TAPE

BOTTOM PIECE

❸ Stand the can inside the boat about 4" (10 cm) from the bow. Gently curve the front ends of the sides around it so they meet. Don't force the wood; move the can back if necessary. Glue and tape the ends together.

Glue and tape the middle of the sides to the bottom.

❹ Place the boat on the cutting board and trim the bottom to fit the bow's shape. Glue and tape the front of the bow to the bottom.

TRIM OFF 4" (10 CM)

(OVERHEAD VIEW)

To build the cabin:

❶ Cut out windows and a door as shown.

CABIN SIDES

CABIN FRONT

WINDOWS

DOOR

Tape the five CABIN pieces (FRONT, two SIDES, TOP, and BACK) together.

Place the cabin on the boat to check its fit; trim and retape if necessary. Glue the cabin together, then glue and tape it to the boat.

CABIN TOP

CABIN BACK

❷ Make two long open boxes from the CABIN LOCKER pieces. Put aside to dry.

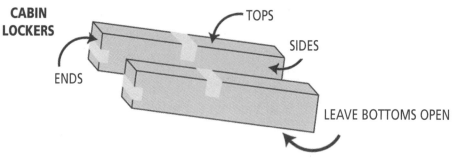

CABIN LOCKERS

TOPS

SIDES

ENDS

LEAVE BOTTOMS OPEN

To build the long lockers:

❶ Glue and tape each LONG LOCKER TOP to a LONG LOCKER SIDE as shown.

❷ Glue them to the boat.

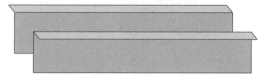

LONG LOCKER SIDES & TOPS

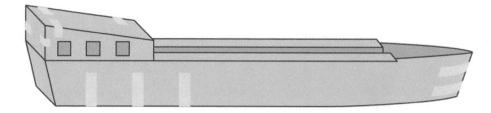

To make the mast:

❶ From the ¼" x ¼" (5 mm x 5 mm) balsa stick, cut a MAST 11" (27.5 cm) long and a CROSSPIECE 9" (23 cm) long. Mark the middle of the crosspiece; straighten one end of one small paper clip and stick it through the crosspiece. Then, stick it through the mast about 2" (5 cm) from one end so the crosspiece can swing back and forth and bend the end down to secure it.

❷ Cut a notch in the balsa block the same width as the mast.

2" (5 CM)

MAST DETAIL

To assemble your model:

(refer to the illustration of the finished keelboat):

❶ When the glue is dry, remove all tape. Put the boat upside down on the cutting board and trim off the part of the long lockers that hangs over the sides.

❷ Slip the rectangular FRONT DECK piece under the bow. Trace the bow and mark where the long lockers begin. Cut out the FRONT DECK. With the boat right side up, glue and tape the deck to the boat.

BALSA BLOCK

FRONT DECK

THIN BALSA STICK FOR KEEL

❸ Glue and tape the balsa block 6" (15 cm) back from the bow, with the notch facing the stern. Glue and tape the cabin lockers, open side down, to the top of the cabin.

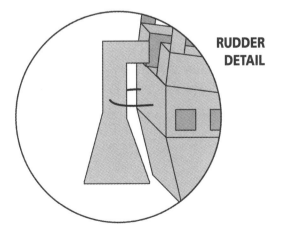

RUDDER DETAIL

❹ Turn the boat onto one side. Glue and tape the thin balsa stick along the middle of the bottom from the stern to the point of the bow; trim as needed. (This is the *keel*, or spine, of the boat. In a real boat, it's put on first.)

Let everything dry, then remove all tape.

❺ Straighten the other small paper clip and bend it into a U shape. Use it to attach the rudder to the stern. Trim to fit if necessary.

Put the mast in (if it's loose, wrap it with masking tape). See how you can lower it by swinging it back? Hang the cloth from the crosspiece with the two large paper clips, and tie the mast and sail to the boat with string or thread.

Although this boat may not float for long, if you decide to try it, please ask an adult for permission and supervision if infants or toddlers are nearby.

TRY IT!

The Corps' keelboat had an awning on top of the cabin like the canopy of a covered wagon. Can you think of a way to put one on your boat? You can also add benches for the oarsmen.

A REPRODUCTION KEELBOAT FLOATING BY THE DOCK ON BLUE LAKE (FORMERLY PART OF THE MISSOURI RIVER) AT LEWIS AND CLARK STATE PARK IN ONAWA, IOWA

A Busy Start

Yes, Jefferson seems to have made an excellent choice in Lewis. He has put a tremendous amount of effort into organizing this expedition, and he is eagerly learning the new and necessary skills. But it seems that Lewis has also made some very important decisions, which perhaps Jefferson could not have anticipated!

EQUAL PARTNERS

As Lewis was preparing for the expedition, he realized two things that would have a huge impact on the trip and how it is recounted in history:

* He would need more men than he and President Jefferson had discussed.

* More important, he would need another officer!

The officer had to be someone who could help share Lewis's responsibilities, discipline the men, and take over for him if he were injured or killed. It had to be a man Lewis knew well, trusted, and could get along with in good times and bad. Lewis thought immediately of his old friend, William Clark.

An Invitation to Greatness

June 19, 1803

You are -invited- to join our EXPEDITION* *bring your own boat

Meriwether Lewis wrote to Clark, mentioning their "long and uninterrupted friendship" and explaining his plan "to descend the Ohio [River] in a keeled boat thence up the Mississippi" to the Missouri, and up that river to the Columbia if possible, and "by descending it reach the Western Ocean." Then he asked Clark to join him as an equal partner with duties and honors that "in all respects be precisely such as my own." Lewis added, "Believe me there is no man on earth with whom I should feel equal pleasure in sharing them as with yourself."

It took almost a month for the letter to reach Clark and another 10 days for Lewis to receive Clark's acceptance. The letter was, according to noted historian Donald Jackson, "one of the most famous invitations to greatness." It launched a great partnership and a grand adventure.

Meriwether Lewis: Curious and Courageous

Meriwether Lewis was born August 18, 1774, at his family's plantation in Virginia (near Jefferson's plantation). Meriwether hardly knew his father, who died when his son was 5, but was very close to his mother, Lucy. She was known for her herbal medicines and doctoring ways. And she was brave. When British soldiers burst into her home during the Revolutionary War, she grabbed a rifle and chased them out!

After Lucy remarried, the family moved to a colony on the Georgia frontier. Only 8, Meriwether hunted raccoons at night alone with his dogs and spent his days exploring the woods. He'd come home to his mother with all sorts of questions. Lucy taught her son about nature, herbs, and how to tend the sick, and maybe about courage, too. One night, when Meriwether was 10, Indians attacked the colony. The whites fled into the woods to hide, but then one man started a fire. The Indians saw it and shot in that direction. As the adults panicked, a calm, quick-thinking Meriwether poured water over the fire. Once again darkness hid them and the Indians went away.

At 13, Meriwether returned to Virginia to study. He was good at math, geography, nature, and science (but not spelling!). He loved to read explorers' journals. After his stepfather died, Meriwether brought his family back to their home in Virginia. Managing the plantation was a big job for an 18-year-old, but even so he got bored. Eventually he joined the U.S. Army and became a paymaster (the officer who distributes soldiers' wages) along the Ohio River. That's when he learned all about keelboats (pages 16–22) and traveling on rivers.

Lieutenant Clark, Sir!

Can you believe that bad behavior brought Lewis and Clark together? Lewis's first position as an Army officer was under General Anthony Wayne at Fort Greenville on the Ohio frontier. One night after drinking too much, Lewis insulted another officer and challenged him to a duel. Because dueling was against Army rules, Lewis was brought up on charges. But General Wayne let Lewis off easy. He transferred Lewis to a company of sharpshooters (riflemen known for their excellent aim) led by none other than Lieutenant William Clark. So Clark actually started off as Lewis's boss! During the next six months, the two men became friends and developed a deep respect for each other.

> "I will chearfully join you … My friend I do assure you that no man lives whith whome I would prefur to undertake Such a Trip."
>
> —*William Clark to Meriwether Lewis, letter, July 18, 1803*

"Chearfully"?

You'll note many unusual spellings in the journal excerpts throughout this book. We have decided to show you the words exactly as they were written by the people at the time, even if they are spelled incorrectly.

How many spelling errors can you find in the excerpt from Clark's letter?

William Clark: Cool and Competent

Redheaded William Clark was born August 1, 1770, in Virginia, the ninth of 10 children. When Billy was 14, the family crossed the Appalachians and traveled down the Ohio River, settling in Louisville, Kentucky. Billy's older brother General George Rogers Clark lived across the river in Clarksville, in Indiana Territory. George had been a hero in the Revolutionary War (yes, the town was named after him) and was now fighting Indians. Settlers coming into this area threatened the Indians' hunting grounds, and there were many raids back and forth.

Billy had little formal schooling, but George taught him about nature and living in the wilderness. The boy became an expert hunter and woodsman, and developed skills with riverboats as

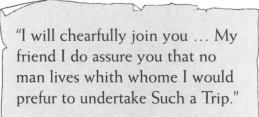

well. At 19, William joined the Kentucky militia (citizens organized to fight as soldiers) to help protect settlers from Indians in the Ohio River Valley. After three years of fighting and helping to negotiate with Indians, William (no more nicknames for the big six-footer!) earned the rank of lieutenant in the U.S. Army. He led the company of sharpshooters that Meriwether later joined in a battle against the Shawnee (shaw-NEE) Indians.

Known for his courage and resourcefulness, William was a good leader. Although he drilled his men hard, he took time to get to know and understand them. He was also good at drawing maps, surveying land, and building forts. After William quit the Army, he settled with George in Clarksville. It was there that Clark received Lewis's invitation.

answer: Four misspellings: "chearfully" should be cheerfully; "whith"/with, "whome"/whom, "prefur"/prefer.

0 1021 0164114 4

Two Captains?

To make sure Clark was his equal in every way on the expedition, Lewis asked that Clark be made a captain, too. The War Department (the branch of the United States government that oversaw the Army at that time) refused. Although Clark would be paid as a captain, he would remain a lieutenant. Lewis was furious and refused to accept the decision. He promised Clark that the expedition's men would never know he was not a captain. And they never did. They called both Lewis and Clark "Captain" and considered them co-commanders.

Lewis and Clark shared some qualities. They even looked a bit alike. But they were different, too. Lewis could be awkward among people. Sometimes he was moody, and he may have suffered from depression at times. Clark was good-natured. He enjoyed talking with his men around the campfire. Their different skills led them to do different jobs on the expedition. Lewis served as the naturalist — collecting, preserving, and describing animals and plants. Clark, in turn, drew most of the maps and organized the boats' packing and unpacking. Amazingly, during the 28 months of the expedition, the two men, it is said, never argued.

THINK ABOUT IT

Why Lewis Made Clark an Equal Partner

If you were given sole command of an expedition by the president, would you choose another person to be your co-leader? After all, in most cases, there's only one boss, right? What Lewis did was extraordinary. But we'll never know for sure why he did it, because neither man wrote about the reasons.

Historians figure it's because Lewis wanted Clark to join the expedition so much that he offered him the partnership to make certain Clark would accept. As it turned out, it was a great decision. Do you think it was a risky decision at the time?

> "The day after tomorrow I shall set out for the Western Country. I feel myself perfectly prepared."
>
> —Meriwether Lewis to his mother, letter, July 2, 1803

Getting Along

Never arguing is difficult even in the best of times, but under trying circumstances such as the Corps faced, it sounds downright unbelievable. But even if Lewis and Clark did disagree occasionally, apparently they were able to get along very well. What makes it even more unusual is that they had equal power, which means neither one had to obey the other. So, how'd they do it?

You probably have some ideas from your own experiences with your friends. Think about when you argue and when you don't. A few things that might have helped Lewis and Clark (or you and your friends) are:

- **Having clearly defined, agreed-upon responsibilities.** This means that they each had a job to do so they weren't arguing about who gets to do what.

- **Having different abilities.** When two people have different skills that they are good at, each one has an opportunity to excel in his own area, plus they aren't competing against each other. In fact, they *want* the other person to do well!

- **Respecting each other.** Respect is different from liking someone. When you respect someone, it means that you admire something about that person's character and the way that person handles particular situations.

Are these some of the factors that help you and your friends get along together, or are there other reasons?

Troubles and Delays

July 5, 1803
Pittsburgh, Pennsylvania

Lewis spent much of June 1803 with Jefferson in Washington discussing his instructions. On July 5, Lewis left for Pittsburgh. He expected that when he arrived, the keelboat, supplies, and soldiers who were assigned to him would be ready. He planned to head down the Ohio River immediately, picking up William Clark along the way. But the keelboat wasn't ready. The builder had been drinking too much, and he hadn't gotten the work done!

First the trip was delayed days, and then weeks, causing Lewis to worry about the water level in the Ohio River. He was concerned that it would dry up under the hot summer sun and get too low for the keelboat. He begged, threatened, and yelled at the boat builder. (Guess he doesn't get along with everyone!)

August 31, 1803

Finally, just four hours after the last nail was hammered into place on the last day of August, Lewis and his men loaded the supplies and launched the keelboat. Lewis had been right to worry. The Ohio was too low for the keelboat. Even though Lewis used extra pirogues and shipped some supplies by wagon, he and the men often had to unload and lift the boat over *sandbars*, the shallow areas created where the river current deposits sand. That had to be a tough way to finally get started!

To Camp Wood

October 15, 1803

On October 15, Lewis met up with Clark in Clarksville. There, the two captains took on more men and Clark decided that his slave, York, would come, too. The expedition continued down the Ohio to the Mississippi River. But as soon as they turned up the mighty Mississippi, the captains realized they would need more muscle power. They were going upstream against the current and would continue upstream once they were headed up the Missouri as well. As they inched their way past an Army post and small settlements of mostly French Canadians and Spaniards, they recruited more volunteers.

The expedition continued down the Ohio, reaching the Mississippi on November 13. There Lewis practiced taking readings for latitude and longitude, and Clark did his first survey. He measured the distance across both rivers — the Ohio was 1,274 yards (1,147 m) wide and the Mississippi was 1,435 yards (1,292 m) wide.

December 12, 1803
Camp Wood

Finally, on a gloomy December day (more than three months since Lewis had left Pittsburgh), they stopped at Wood River, just north of St. Louis and right across from the mouth of the Missouri. There, under cottonwoods, maples, and oaks, they built a cluster of sturdy log cabins — quarters for the men and the captains, one for blacksmithing, plus a storehouse. They called it Camp Wood.

Go with the Flow!

A river flows *downstream* from its *source*, which is usually a stream in the mountains, to its *mouth*, the place where the river flows into another larger river or into the ocean. So when the Corps was headed up the Mississippi, and eventually, the Missouri as well, they were traveling *upstream* against the current, which made it very difficult, indeed!

DO A LAND SURVEY

When Clark used his surveying equipment to measure the width of the rivers, he was using triangles to determine distance. Even the most advanced instruments we have today that use satellites to measure positions on earth are based on triangles.

You can also use triangles to determine the distance between two points, just as Clark learned to do before the expedition. Ask a friend to help you use this equipment and take the measurements.

Supplies

- Protractor
- Pencil
- 12" x 12" (30 x 30 cm) piece of stiff cardboard
- Ruler

- Thumbtack
- Tape
- Large drinking straw
- String or cord, at least 11' (3.3 m)

- Two poles or sticks (at eye level or shorter)
- Graph paper
- Carpenter's tape measure

To make your surveying instruments:

❶ You'll need a larger version of the protractor. Here's how to make one: Using the protractor, mark the center point, baseline (0°), and every 10° up to 90° on the cardboard. Extend and label the lines to make one-half of a jumbo protractor (a quarter-circle).

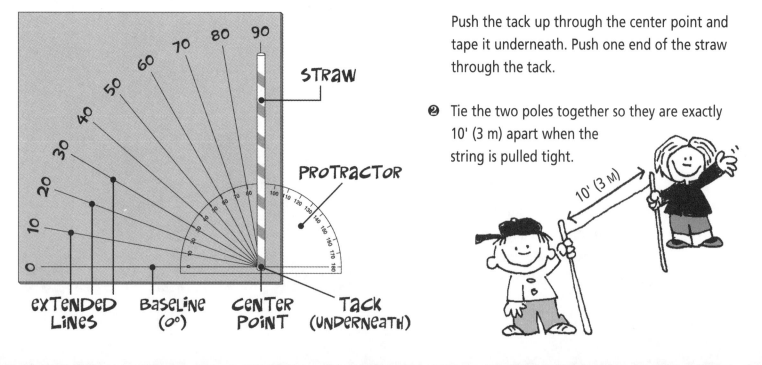

Push the tack up through the center point and tape it underneath. Push one end of the straw through the tack.

❷ Tie the two poles together so they are exactly 10' (3 m) apart when the string is pulled tight.

To measure the angles:

❶ Choose two points and stick one pole into the
ground at Point A. Place your jumbo protractor
on the pole at the tack. Move the straw so it lines
up with the 0° line. Holding the protractor level,
move it so you can see Point B through the straw.

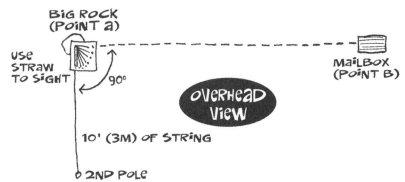

❷ Now move the straw so it lines up along 90°. Without
moving the protractor, look through the straw. Direct
your partner to hold the other pole where you can see it through the straw. The string should be stretched tight.

❸ Double-check that Point A is still at 0° and the other
pole is at 90°. Then have your partner push the
second pole into the ground at that spot.

❹ Place the jumbo protractor on the second pole. With
the string at 0° as the baseline, sight Point B through
the straw and determine the angle. Record it.

To calculate the distance:

❶ Next, you'll draw a right triangle based on your measurements.
Near the bottom of the graph paper, draw a horizontal line
10 squares long. At the left end, draw a long vertical line at a
right angle to it. Now, at the right end, use your protractor to
construct the angle you determined in step 4 above. Extend a
line at that angle until it crosses the line at the left.

❷ Each square on the paper is equal to 1' (30 cm). Count how many
squares make up the vertical line and multiply by 1' (30 cm). That's
the distance between Points A and B.

❸ So, how good at surveying are you? Measure the distance between
the two points with the tape measure to find out.

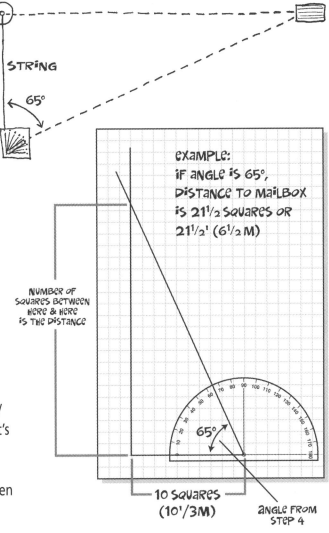

MEET THE CORPS

If you were Lewis or Clark, what characteristics and skills would you look for in the men you recruited? Both Lewis and Clark knew that the success of the expedition depended on the men they chose, as much as on their own leadership. It depended on whether they could shape those men into a close-knit group who would look out for each other, using their individual talents and skills for the good of the group and the expedition's success.

But what challenges and hardships would the recruits have to meet? Lewis and Clark already knew about the first leg of the journey, up the Missouri to the Mandan Indian villages. Fur traders had been going up and down that part of the river for years. Rowing upstream would be difficult, and the captains anticipated that they could run into trouble with at least one American Indian tribe, the Teton Sioux (TEE-ton SOO), also known as Lakota (la-KO-tah) (page 52). They were known to be hostile to whites as well as to other Indians. As for the rest of the way to the Pacific, the territory was largely unknown and the Indian nations were mostly unfamiliar.

Good thing they were staying the winter at Camp Wood, just north of St. Louis. They would have time to judge each man's temperament and skill levels carefully and learn what they could about the area west of the Mandan villages.

Selecting the Men

Before they met in Clarksville, Lewis had written Clark that he should be looking for "good hunters, stout, healthy, unmarried men, accustomed to the woods, and capable of bearing bodily fatigue." Men who knew carpentry or blacksmithing would also be useful. Clark agreed. The partners were already working well together.

As word got out about the expedition, young men who wanted to join pestered Lewis and Clark. No one, it seemed, could resist such an adventure! In Clarksville, the captains were overwhelmed when more than 100 young frontiersmen volunteered. Clark rejected "several young Gentlemens sons" because they were not rugged enough.

So Lewis and Clark could pick and choose their Corps from many eager volunteers. They tested the men's shooting and hunting abilities and asked about special skills. They judged whether each man had the physical strength and character for a long, hard journey. Would this man accept discipline? Would that one stick with the expedition through difficult times? Yes, there was a lot to think about in the selection process, because how the men functioned together could make or break the expedition.

Building a Team at Camp Wood

Over the winter, Lewis traveled frequently to St. Louis to make more preparations. Back at Camp Wood, Clark practiced with his surveying instruments (learning to take the measurements he would use to draw maps), started a weather log, and trained the 40 or so men who had been chosen so far. Every day the men practiced shooting, which they really liked. They also did military drills (organized practices of marching), which were not popular. They hunted and they chopped wood. When bored and restless, some of the men fought. One night, Sergeant John Ordway (page 35) was left in charge while Lewis and Clark were both gone. Four men went off and got drunk; others refused to obey Ordway's orders to stand guard. Did Lewis and Clark dismiss these men? No.

Clark had confidence in his and Lewis's choices, or at least in their ability to bring the men together to make a team. After all, these volunteers were mostly a mix of rough soldiers from wilderness posts (remote Army stations), Kentucky frontiersmen, and French-Canadian boatmen, who were accustomed to a loose, undisciplined lifestyle. The captains knew to expect misbehavior early on and punished wrongdoers with lectures about security, extra work, or confinement to quarters (that's like being grounded). Gradually, the men began working better together, although they still grumbled about boring jobs like making sugar, gathering honey, and pounding dried corn into meal.

Organizing the Corps of Discovery

In a ceremony on March 31, 1804, Lewis and Clark appointed John Ordway, Charles Floyd, and Nathaniel Pryor "Sergeants with equal Powers" and divided 22 more men into three squads under them. Although the expedition's purpose was not to conquer people or land, it was a military operation. Men not already in the U.S. Army were sworn in. From now on everyone was expected to obey orders and accept military punishment.

These 25 soldiers were assigned the task of handling the keelboat up the Missouri to the Mandan villages. They all expected to continue traveling to the Pacific Ocean. Along the way, however, some of the men would leave, while other people, including the Shoshone woman Sacagawea (page 57) and her baby, would join. Also going all the way were York and George Drouillard, an interpreter. In the end 33 people plus one dog — Lewis's big, black Newfoundland, Seaman, that he bought in Pittsburgh for $20 — went to the Pacific and back. These 33 were called the Permanent Party.

In addition to the Permanent Party, seven more soldiers and about ten boatmen hired in St. Louis came along. The plan was to have these men travel only as far as the Mandan villages, then return in the keelboat with specimens, maps, and reports. How disappointing to be chosen for this group — but better than not being selected at all!

The Permanent Party Roster

Captain Meriwether Lewis
Captain William Clark
York
Sergeant Patrick Gass
Sergeant John Ordway
Sergeant Nathaniel Pryor
Private William Bratton
Private John Collins
Private John Colter
Private Pierre Cruzatte

Private Joseph Field
Private Reuben Field
Private Robert Frazer
Private George Gibson
Private Silas Goodrich
Private Hugh Hall
Private Thomas Howard
Private François Labiche
Private Jean Baptiste
    LePage

Private Hugh McNeal
Private John Potts
Private George Shannon
Private John Shields
Private John Thompson
Private Peter Weiser
Private William Werner
Private Joseph Whitehouse
Private Alexander Willard
Private Richard Windsor

George Drouillard
    (interpreter)
Toussaint Charbonneau
    (interpreter)
Sacagawea
Jean Baptiste "Pomp"
    Charbonneau

woof!

Meet the Permanent Party

The Permanent Party was a melting pot of sorts. It included Americans of different backgrounds and heritage, a German immigrant, French Canadians, French-Canadian Indians, and a black man. Let's meet some of them.

My name's **Sergeant Patrick Gass,** 33, from Pennsylvania. I was a *private* (lowest-ranking Army officer) until the others elected me to replace Charles Floyd after he died (pages 49–50). Before I entered the Army, I was a carpenter, so I help build our winter quarters and make dugout canoes. I also keep a journal.

I'm **Sergeant John Ordway,** 29, from New Hampshire, a soldier from the 1st Infantry Regiment. The captains put me in charge when they're both away. My duties include issuing *provisions* (food) and appointing guard duties. I keep a journal and other records for the expedition.

I'm **Private Pierre Cruzatte** (creu-ZAT), expert boatman and fur trader. Even though I'm missing one eye, I know the Missouri River like the back of my hand. The son of French and Omaha (OH-ma-ha) Indian parents, I speak Omaha and know Indian signs, so I help translate. I love entertaining the men with my fiddle.

I'm **Private John Shields,** 35, a blacksmith from Kentucky, where I've got a wife and daughter. Guess it was my skill at repairing guns and my promise to do better that kept the captains from kicking me out of Camp Wood when I disobeyed Sergeant Ordway.

I'm **Sergeant Nathaniel Hale Pryor,** a Kentuckian born in Virginia. At 32 and one of the only two married men, I'm more responsible than some of the other Corps members, so the captains often ask me to do things like invite Indian tribal leaders to *council* (meeting) and head a *court-martial* (military trial).

Please?

I'm **Private Reuben Field,** 32, and this here's my brother **Joseph**, 30. We came to Kentucky from Virginia. We're woodsmen and hunters, and can find our way any-where. The captains often use us as scouts on dangerous and difficult missions. I'm lucky to be here after that Ordway incident.

My name's **Private George Shannon,** from Pennsylvania. I'm 19, the youngest in the Corps. I'm real proud they made me second in command in Sergeant Pryor's squad and named a stream off the Yellowstone River, Shannon's Creek, after me!

I'm the interpreter, **George Drouillard**. I'm 29. My father is French-Canadian and my mother is Shawnee, so I'm familiar with Indian ways. In addition to English, I speak French and several Indian languages, and I'm also good at Indian sign language (page 79). I'm proud to say that Captain Lewis thinks I'm the best hunter and scout.

Oui!

I'm **York,** about the same age as Captain Clark. I've been his slave since we were boys. As his manservant, I'm used to going where he goes. I'm good at hunting and trapping, and at trading with Indians, too, as it turns out. I'm the first black man they've ever seen, and my color, size, and strength amaze and sometimes frighten them.

My name's **Private John Colter,** about 30, I think, and born in Virginia, though I've been a Kentuckian since I was little. I love adventure and sometimes get into trouble. The captains were real nice to assign me to the Permanent Party even after I disobeyed the sergeant.

"fixing for a Start"

With Lewis in St. Louis making final preparations, it was up to Clark and the sergeants to get the expedition underway from Camp Wood.

After local settlers told Clark the Teton Sioux were well armed, he had the men mount a cannon at the bow of the keelboat on a swivel so it could turn in any direction. They also installed *blunderbusses* (shotguns with short, flared muzzles) on swivels in the keelboat and pirogues, and built new benches and storage lockers. The lockers' lids could be raised for protection during an attack. Each man was also armed with a rifle or a musket (page 15).

After packing the supplies in large bundles, carefully marking each one, Clark spent a week experimenting with different ways to load the boats to make it easiest to move them through the water. On May 13, 1804, he sent a message to Lewis. The boats, he wrote, were "Complete with Sails … men, all in health and readiness to set out."

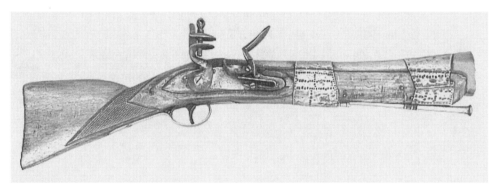

BLUNDERBUSS

The "Writingest Explorers"

Lewis brought paper, ink, pencils, and "Creyons" (as he spelled it) and a heavy four-volume dictionary. Why? Because President Jefferson wanted Lewis and Clark to keep journals. Lewis began his back in August 1803 on that first day on the Ohio River, complaining that he "was much fatiegued after labouring with my men all day." Much of what we know about the expedition comes from the captains' and other men's journals. Historians have called them "a priceless gift," and Lewis and Clark the "writingest explorers." Throughout this book you'll get to see what the men saw, hear what they heard, and feel what they felt in their own words, in the "Travel with the Corps" journal excerpts.

You can even discover through their writing how different the two leaders were. Lewis used words to paint vivid pictures of scenery, animals, and plants. But weeks, even months, would pass when he didn't write at all. No one knows why. There's no mention of lost journals; perhaps he was too busy or too tired. Clark, on the other hand, wrote nearly every day. His writing is more direct and practical, just as he was.

TRY IT!

If you enjoy journaling, then now is the time to begin one! You can write about so many things: If you are interested in people, write your opinions about how the people on the expedition behaved or your observations about how people were treated. Do you like nature? Borrow a book from the library or go on the Internet and look up some of the animals and plants that are mentioned along the way. Keep your own journal about what the members of the expedition observed, noting where it was seen in case you get to that part of the country some day. Are you interested in geography? Hunting and fishing? Drawing and sketching? American Indian history? There are so many different ways for you to bring your interests and your expertise along on this expedition, so go to it!

Mystery of the Missing Journals

Lewis reported to Jefferson that seven men were writing journals, in addition to Clark and himself. Journals from Sergeants Ordway, Floyd, and Gass survived. If Sergeant Pryor also kept a journal, as he was supposed to, it's never been found — yet! But keep looking — parts of Private Joseph Whitehouse's journals weren't found until 1966!

Travel with the Corps

May 14, 1804 (Day 1 of the Expedition)
21 miles (33.8 km)

On that May morning, Clark wrote in his journal, "fixing for a Start." But as Patrick Gass noted, "the day was showery" and they had to wait until late afternoon before pushing their boats into the mouth of the Missouri. Wrote Clark: "I determined to go as far as St. Charles, a french Village 7 Leags [leagues; a *league* is about 3 miles/4.8 km] up the Missourie, and wait at that place untill Capt. Lewis could join me by Land … I set out at 4 oClock P.M., in the presence of many of the Neighbouring inhabitants, and proceeded on under a jentle brease up the Missourie and Camped on the [first] Island."

UP THE MISSOURI

As soon as the Corps of Discovery left St. Charles, the men realized the Missouri River would test all their skills, strengths, and resourcefulness. The river was a bucking bronco one moment and a stubborn mule the next. Its swift, strong current tore whole trees out of the riverbanks. Branches racing downstream rammed into the boats, oars snapped on rocks and the mast hit an overhead branch and broke. Whirlpools sucked at the boats and rapids almost tipped them over. Then a sandbar would suddenly appear and one of the boats would inevitably become stuck.

With their eyes peeled for hazards ahead, while constantly shouting warnings to the others, Pierre Cruzatte or François Labiche (la-BEESH) rode in the bow of the keelboat at all times. Like Cruzatte (page 35), Labiche was half Omaha, half French, and an excellent boatman. If the wind was in the right direction, the crew raised the sail. Mostly they rowed or, using long poles, pushed the keelboat while walking along the tops of the lockers on the boat's sides. Often they had to tow the boat by hand from the muddy shore. It was a bit easier for the men on the pirogues because those vessels were lighter and smaller. But progress against the current was slow no matter which boat, and there were many delays.

You're in the Army Now!

As a military expedition, the Corps of Discovery had strict rules of conduct. Once the journey was underway, Lewis and Clark had to maintain a well-disciplined unit of soldiers, ready to respond to the unknown challenges that lay ahead. Getting drunk or sleeping on duty put all of the men in danger. Flogging with a whip made of nine knotted cords (called a cat-o'-nine-tails) was a common punishment in the Army back then. Under the rules of war, stealing a blanket called for 50 lashes and sitting down on guard duty warranted 100. You could be put to death for sleeping on duty or deserting (leaving permanently without permission)!

The men got an early indication of how seriously Lewis and Clark regarded these offenses. While still in St. Charles, John Collins and two other Corps members were accused of being "absent without leave" after a village dance. Collins was also charged with being disrespectful to an officer. The captains put Sergeant Ordway in charge of a court-martial and named four privates to the jury. They found all three guilty and sentenced Collins to 50 lashes on his back and the others to 25 each.

Despite that painful punishment, two of those same men got drunk a month later, this time on guard duty. They were court-martialed, with Sergeant Pryor in charge, and again found guilty and whipped. Three weeks later, Ordway caught another private sleeping while on guard duty. This time the captains acted as the jury. Found guilty, he received 100 lashes, delivered over four days.

Travel with the Corps

May 28, 1804 (Day 15)

It "rained hard all the last night," according to Clark on May 28, 1804, "and [got] Several articles Wet." Two days later with the "current verry Swift," there was "a heavy wind accompanied with rain & hail." The next day, "the wind blew with great force which obliged us to lay by [wait before traveling on]."

THINK ABOUT IT

Judged by Your Peers

When Lewis and Clark decided to have a court-martial in which one of the privates was judged – not by the captains – but by a group of fellow privates, they did something that was common in civilian life but unheard of in the military back then. They held a trial by a jury of one's peers (equals) 150 years before the U. S. Army did. And then they had the men, instead of the officers, administer the punishment.

Why? They were still building the men into team players who would look out for each other in the wilderness. They also wanted to forge a bond with their men. Imagine if you were a member of the Corps and were asked to be on a court-martial jury. Would you feel honored by the captains? Or would the responsibility be too much for you? If the person on trial was a buddy, would you vote "not guilty" no matter what the evidence showed? What if you were on trial? Would you prefer being judged by your peers?

st Did They Travel?

Typically, the Corps traveled 6 to 12 miles (9.5 to 19 km) a day going up the Missouri, depending on the conditions. On a really good day, with the wind coming from behind, the keelboat could cover 20 miles (32 km) in a day. (A day might be anywhere from four hours to 10 hours, depending on length of daylight and other factors.) After the expedition left the keelboat and was traveling by pirogues (page 16) and dugouts, the pace picked up some, but these boats were often slowed down by blowing sand and windstorms.

Using a Compass

A *magnetic compass* is a simple device used to determine direction. It has a small magnet, called the needle, which swings on a pivot. One end of the needle is colored or marked N for north. Compasses also have a directional arrow and a dial. Letters and degrees (just like on a protractor, page 30) on the dial indicate north (0°), east (90°), south (180°), and west (270°), and all directions between.

No matter where you are on earth, the north end of the needle will point toward the North Pole. That's because the earth itself is a gigantic magnet, with the south end of its magnet at the North Pole and the north end at the South Pole (remember, with magnets, opposites attract!).

If you don't have a compass at home, you can buy a small one at a sporting goods store for a couple of dollars. (Or, for directions on how to make a simple one, check at the library for *The Kids' Science Book* by Hirschfeld and White or on the web at <**www.howstuffworks.com/ compass.html**>.)

Measuring Distance: Dead Reckoning

Measuring distance traveled based on latitude and longitude and surveying with triangles was much too complicated for mapping all the twists and turns in the river. Instead, Clark estimated distances using dead reckoning.

❶ Before starting, Clark noted the time. He looked ahead to the next bend in the river or landmark and took a compass reading to determine its direction.

❷ Once underway, Clark determined the speed of the boat with a *log line:* A weighted piece of wood (the *log*) was tied to the end of a rope (the *line*) whose length was evenly marked with knots every 42' (12.6 m) apart. Clark would throw the log overboard and then count the number of knots that passed over the boat's rail in 30 seconds as the boat traveled away from the log. That number of knots was the boat's speed in *knots*, or nautical miles per hour.

If Clark were walking, he'd use his walking speed, which he knew from experience.

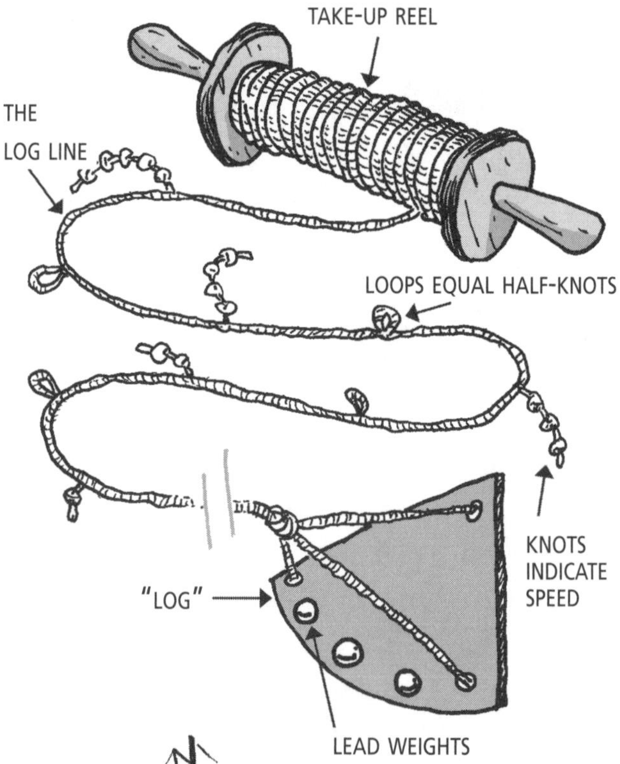

❸ When Clark reached the next bend or landmark, he noted the time again and double-checked his earlier compass reading. To calculate the distance traveled, he multiplied the boat's speed (or his walking speed) by the amount of time that had passed. Then he sighted another landmark upriver and repeated the whole process.

❹ Clark kept track of all these distances and changes in direction in his journal. He also sketched the river's course, as well as features like islands, streams, and sandbars.

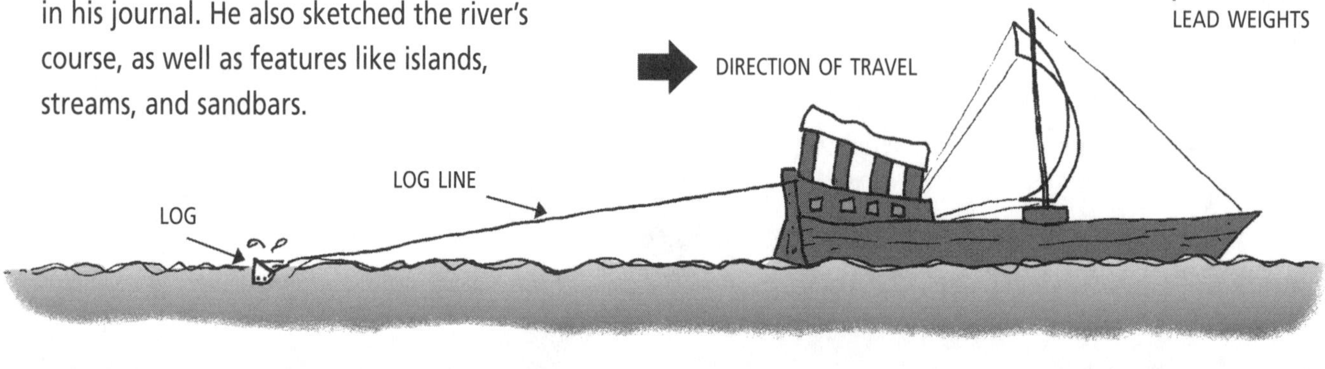

TAKE-UP REEL

THE LOG LINE

LOOPS EQUAL HALF-KNOTS

KNOTS INDICATE SPEED

"LOG"

LEAD WEIGHTS

DIRECTION OF TRAVEL

LOG LINE

LOG

CAN YOU DEAD RECKON?

By the time the Corps of Discovery reached the Pacific Ocean, William Clark estimated it had traveled 4,162 miles (6,697 km) along the twisting course from Camp Wood. By one account he was off by only 40 miles (64 km). Considering his equipment, that's amazing! Would you be that good at dead reckoning? Try this game with some friends and see.

Supplies

➤ Paper and pencils
➤ Carpenter's tape measure
➤ Watch with second hand or a stopwatch
➤ Compass
➤ Your surveying instruments (pages 30–31)

To choose a site:

❶ Outdoors, lay out a zigzag course, with three to five legs, or sections. Keep each leg fairly short (no more than 20 giant steps) because you'll be measuring them later on. The landmarks that mark the beginning and end of each leg must be permanent (don't use a sleeping dog that will wake up and walk away!).

So *that's* what a knot is!

If you sail or read about sailing, you've surely heard the term *knots*, referring to a boat's speed. Now that you have read about Clark's calculations, the term means a lot more. Once Clark knew the number of knots, he could calculate feet per minute or land miles per hour. (A nautical mile is 6,076 feet, or 1,852 m/1.85 km, a little bit longer than a mile when measured on land.) Imagine keeping track of this constantly while traveling in sometimes wild, oftentimes dangerous conditions!

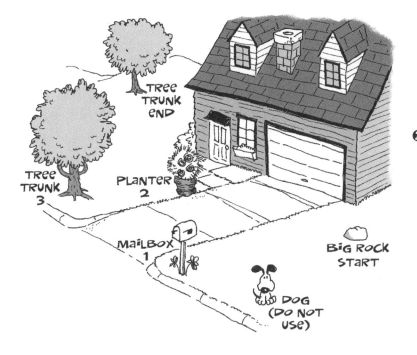

❷ Roughly sketch the course and label the landmarks Start, 1, 2, 3, and End. Note what the landmarks are.

To determine each player's walking speed:

Measure the distance from Start to Landmark 1. Time how many seconds it takes for each player to walk this leg, walking at normal speed. Divide the distance by the number of seconds. This gives you each person's walking speed in feet per second (or meters per second). Record the result. (To get a more accurate estimate of your speed, clock the first leg several times and average the readings by adding up the times and dividing by the number of readings you took.)

To measure the course:

Now, each player takes a turn walking the course with the compass and watch.
Each is responsible for taking her own readings, but it's easier if someone else comes along to record them.

❶ At Start, take a compass reading to determine the direction to Landmark 1. Record the reading in degrees from north. (If you're using a homemade compass, estimate the degrees.) Time yourself as you walk to the landmark and record the number of seconds. Next, take a compass reading for Landmark 2, then walk and time the second leg. Repeat until you reach the End.

❷ When finished, each player uses her own walking speed and times to calculate the length of each leg. If your walking speed is 2' (.6 m) per second, for example, and it took you 15 seconds to walk the first leg, the first leg is 30' or 9 m (2' per second x 15 seconds = 30' or .6 m per second x 15 seconds = 9 m).

❸ Compare one another's compass readings and distance estimates. If any of them differ by a lot, you might want to go around the course again and retake them. Add the directions and distances to your sketch.

❹ Now, see who's best at dead reckoning! Measure the actual distances of the other legs with the tape measure or your surveying instruments. If your estimates are off by a lot, remember that there are many things that can go wrong in dead reckoning, like walking faster or slower than your normal speed. Rarely is anyone as good at it as Clark was — but keep trying and you'll get very good, too!

The Daily Routine

Days began at dawn with a breakfast of cold leftovers, as no cooking was allowed during the day because it wasted too much time. Then Drouillard (the interpreter) and a few men rode off on the expedition's two horses, hunting for food, while the others pushed off in the boats. One sergeant was stationed on the bow of the keelboat to watch for Indians and other boats. "Pirogues ahead!" he'd call out as trappers' canoes, piled high with furs, came downstream toward them. Another sergeant managed the sail and directed the oarsmen. The sergeant at the stern steered.

Clark was usually on the keelboat or walking nearby. He took compass readings and measured distances for the maps he was keeping. Lewis often hiked inland, observing animals, gathering plants, and collecting samples of minerals and soil.

Seaman, his dog, trotted by his side. Sometimes the captains stopped at the mouth of a tributary or an island to take readings for determining latitude and longitude, which they also did at each camp. Yes, Lewis and Clark seemed to be eagerly pursuing their assignments given by the president.

At night, the men pitched tents and gathered firewood as the cooks prepared the day's only hot meal. Ordway handed out food and whiskey, and each man saved a portion of dinner for the next day's breakfast and lunch. After supper, the men dried the meat that had been caught that day to make jerky (dried beef), repaired clothes, or carved new oars, while the captains and others wrote in their journals. Some men danced to Cruzatte's fiddle playing. And each night the men took turns at guard duty.

What's for Dinner?

When the hunters came back to camp with animals slung over the horses' backs, it's likely they were met with slaps on the back and great "Hoorays!" Their success meant the men got to dine on huge slabs of deer, elk, or bear meat or a turkey or goose drumstick. Their daily ration of cornmeal or flour would be baked into cornbread or hardtack (a hard biscuit) to go with the meat. When the hunters came back empty-handed, the men were stuck with salt pork, cracked corn, and lard from Lewis's supplies, which were typically cooked into a fatty stew. Fresh vegetables were rarely available, but as the weather warmed up, the men munched on ripe mulberries, cherries, plums, and other fruit from the bushes and trees that lined the riverbanks.

"our dog"

As enthusiastically as the hunters were greeted upon their return, they'd still have lost a popularity contest to Seaman. The big dog caught squirrels swimming across the river, brought down a deer wounded by hunters, and retrieved felled geese and ducks in his giant jaws. On an order from Lewis, Seaman would dive underwater to drive beaver out of their lodges, chasing them to the surface where they could be shot. His barking once saved the sleeping men from a panicked buffalo. More than once he gave "timely notice" of bears. Such a big, black, intelligent dog amazed Indians. One tried to buy him; three others tried to steal him. Best of all, Seaman was cuddly. Imagine running your hand through his thick coat or curling up to his warm body on a lonely, cold night. You couldn't do that with the hunters! No wonder everyone in the Corps called Seaman "our dog."

"Muskeetors," "Musquitors," "Musquetoes"!

No matter how the men spelled the word *mosquitoes* in their journals, these bugs were pests. At night, the air was so thick with them that they'd get into the men's noses and ears. Open your mouth and you might swallow one! Bites itched like crazy and often got infected, sometimes causing a fever. Gnats, fleas, and ticks were also problems. Poor Seaman howled in pain from his bites. The men got some relief by standing in the smoke of the campfire and coating their faces, necks, and arms with thick, gooey animal grease. To sleep, they crawled under the mosquito netting that Lewis had thoughtfully bought back in St. Louis.

A Paradise of Curiosities

July 4, 1804 (Day 52)

On July 4, the captains fired the cannon and named a creek Independence. Surrounding them, wrote Floyd, was "one of the Butifules Prairies I ever Saw open and butifulley Divided with Hills and vallies all presenting themselves." The land was covered "with grass about 4½ feet [1.4 m] high," according to Clark. Three weeks later, the Corps passed the Platte River at latitude 41° north, about 600 miles (965 km) from Camp Wood, and moved onto the Great Plains. This huge area of flat, grassy, treeless terrain stretches across the central western portion of the United States from Texas up into Canada. Here, wrote Clark, the "Prairie is Covered with grass about 10 or 12 Inch [25 to 30 cm] high; soil of good quality."

The land swarmed with animals, including "curiosities" they had never seen before like pronghorn antelope, white pelicans, and coyotes; its streams were filled with fish. Lewis declared, "I do not think I exagerate when I estimated the number of Buffaloe which could be comprehended at one view to amount to 3,000."

The funniest "curiositie" was the prairie dog, which Lewis and Clark first saw on September 7 when they came upon a "Village of Small animals that burrow in the grown [ground]." Clark reported that this "village" covered about 4 acres (1.6 hectares) and had "great numbers of holes on the top of which those little animals Set erect." When alarmed, they'd "Slip into their hole," only to pop out of another some distance away. Lewis called them "barking squrils" because "they bark at you as you approach them, their note being much that of little toy dogs."

The captains wanted to send a prairie dog back to President Jefferson. The men dug into the tunnels, poked long poles into the holes, and even poured water in to flush one out. Finally, they captured one and killed another, which Ordway reported "was cooked for the Capts dinner" — but not before Lewis studied and described it.

BISON   PRAIRIE DOG   PRONGHORN ANTELOPE

SOME ANIMALS THAT WERE SEEN ON THE GREAT PLAINS

BE A NATURALIST

Naturalists study living things in their natural environments. They observe the same animal or plant over a period of time to see how it develops and how it behaves. Like Lewis and Clark, naturalists write down detailed observations, noting what surprises them, and often sketching what they see.

Take a walk (pen and notebook in hand, naturalist-style) in your backyard or, with an adult, in a park. Be on the lookout for a type of animal or plant that you'll be able to observe for a month or longer. Look in fields, woods, and ponds or at a spider busily spinning by a basement window. Visit your observation place frequently. Draw sketches: For an animal, draw how it hunts, changes, cares for its young, protects itself, and where it lives. For a plant, draw what eats it! — and how it develops buds and new leaves, creeps, blooms, and then goes to seed.

Describe what you see scientifically, as if no one had ever seen it before, including colors, shapes, sounds, unusual details, and estimates of size. (But don't ever touch an animal in the wild, no matter how friendly and cute it seems.) Ask yourself why a bush has thorns, a hummingbird's beak is so long, or a deer stands so very still? Being a naturalist is a lot like getting to know someone very well. Pleased to meet you!

Calling "Dr." Lewis

Hard work under the hot sun caused headaches and sun-stroke (fever, dizziness, and collapse caused by too much sun). A poisonous snake bit Joseph Field "on the Side of the foot, which Sweled much," according to Floyd. Clark suffered from painful swollen joints, a condition called *rheumatism*. Bug bites, no vegetables, damp clothes, and unclean drinking water also contributed to the men getting sick. As Clark noted on June 17, "The party is much aflicted with Boils [skin infections] and Several have the Decissentary [*dysentery*, an intestinal disease that causes severe diarrhea], which I contribute [attribute] to the water which is muddy."

"Dr." Lewis cut open the boils and, using a soft cloth, applied poultices of heated crushed elm bark and cornmeal to the wound. He cured Field's snakebite with a poultice of bark and niter (the main ingredient in gunpowder!). Blistered feet were soaked in Epsom salts (the minerals magnesium and sulfur). Accidental poisonings got a dose of ipecac. (The root of a tropical plant, *ipecac* is still used today to make a person vomit.) And just about anyone who got sick received a dose of Rush's Thunderbolts (page 13).

May I offer you some ... "Water millions"?

August 2, 1804 (Day 81)

Along the way to the Platte River, Lewis and Clark wondered where the Indians they'd heard so much about were. As it happened, the tribes of the lower Missouri were off buffalo hunting. Then, on August 2, a small group of Oto (OH-toe) and Missouri (ma-ZOO-ree) came to camp. Being farmers as well as hunters, they brought "Water millions" (Clark's spelling of watermelons!). The captains gave the Indians "some rosted meat, Pork, flour & meal," and invited them to a council.

The next morning when the Oto leaders arrived, the Corps performed the ritual they had developed for meeting new tribes: They demonstrated military drills. In his dress uniform, Lewis gave a speech: "Children ... the great Chief of the Seventeen great nations of America [the 17 states] ... is now your only great father." The captains used the title "Chief" for President Jefferson in the same way white people commonly used it to refer to tribal or village leaders. Lewis explained that because of the council between Jefferson and the Indians' "old fathers" (the French and Spanish), the region now belonged to the U.S. He promised that Jefferson would protect their people and wanted to trade with them. Lewis told the Otos they should be at peace with other tribes and with whites. After Clark handed out gifts, the leaders responded: They agreed to trade, asked for gunpowder to fight the Omaha, and complained about the French!

CAPTAINS LEWIS AND CLARK HOLDING A COUNCIL AS SKETCHED BY PATRICK GASS IN HIS JOURNAL

A Deserter, a Death, and a Lost Man

In mid-August, Private Moses Reed deserted. The timing couldn't have been worse. The expedition was about to enter Sioux territory, where they would need every man for protection. Drouillard found and brought him back. After Reed confessed to desertion and stealing a rifle, he was court-martialed, found guilty, and, as Clark reported, We "Sentenced him to run the Gantlet four times." (That meant Reed had to walk, not run, between two lines of men as each one whipped his bare back.) It was a brutal punishment, but it was better than being shot to death. Reed also lost his place in the Permanent Party.

To add to the Corps' woes, Sergeant Floyd, only 22, was dying, probably of a burst appendix. (Even if he had been in Philadelphia with Dr. Rush taking care of him, it's unlikely Floyd would have survived. The first operation to remove an infected appendix wasn't performed until the 1880s.) Added to that, in late August Private George Shannon was missing. The captains sent men to look for him, but he was nowhere to be found.

Travel with the Corps

Honoring Sergeant Floyd

August 20, 1804 (Day 99)

"Serj. Floyd died," wrote Clark on August 20. "This Man at all times gave us proofs of his firmness and Deturmined resolution to doe Service to his Countrey and honor to himself." Whitehouse reported: "We dug a Grave on the Top of a round Nob [knob] & [buried Floyd] with all the honours of War. We named this Hill Serjeant Floyds bluff."

FLOYD'S BLUFF, SIOUX CITY, IOWA

THINK ABOUT IT

Replacing a Sergeant

Put yourself in the captains' shoes. A sergeant has died. Army rules say you can only promote a private. But you're concerned about the men's morale. They've had to punish one man and bury another. Now, you're about to further break up their newly formed team by selecting one as better than the others to be promoted. What could you do to lift the men's spirits?

Well, if you're thinking creatively like Lewis and Clark, you'll let the men themselves select their new sergeant. And that's exactly what they did! They held an election – the first one west of the Mississippi! Patrick Gass won with 19 votes. He was a popular choice with both the men and the captains – and the men surely felt empowered. A brilliant leadership move!

The Yankton Sioux

August 30, 1804 (Day 109)

You just ran the flag up a makeshift pole and are now standing at attention. Four musicians are coming toward the camp, singing and playing music on drums and rattles. Behind them are five Yankton Sioux (YANK-ton SOO) leaders with eagle feathers in their hair to show they have killed enemies in battle. They're dressed in colorful buffalo robes, moccasins, and leggings. It's time for a council. Captain Lewis begins to speak, and French trader Pierre Dorian translates.

The Yankton leaders knew Dorian, who had joined the expedition on the Missouri River. They told him that the trinkets Lewis had given them were not enough. They had observed the keelboat packed with goods. Wasn't it there for trade? They wanted clothes for their people and guns for protection, and they wanted them — needed them — *now.* Lewis tried to explain that they were explorers, not traders, but the Yanktons did not understand.

Eventually everyone agreed to future trade. Weuche (Handshake) even offered to put together a peace delegation from different Indian tribes the next spring. He asked Dorian to stay with them to help and also to arrange for them to visit the great Washington chief (Jefferson). Lastly, Arcawechar (Half Man) warned Lewis and Clark about the Teton Sioux (page 32): "I fear those nations above [farther north] will not open their ears, and you cannot I fear open them."

TEPEES ON THE GREAT PLAINS

Shannon Found!

September 11, 1804 (Day 121)

Sixteen days after Shannon had disappeared, the keelboat's bowman shouted and pointed to the riverbank. Shannon, who thought the Corps was ahead of him, had run upriver as long as he could. Now, exhausted, he was sitting on the bank waiting for a trader's boat. "He had been 12 days without any thing to eate but Grapes & one Rabit" since running out of bullets, wrote Clark, and nearly "Starved to death in a land of Plenty." You can see why Lewis and Clark had made sure to choose healthy men with good wilderness skills.

The Sioux Nations

The Sioux hunted the buffalo herds on the plains. They lived in tepees, which were easy to put up, take down, and transport as needed to follow their seasonal food supplies.

* The **Yankton** or **Nakota Sioux** (na-KO-tah) lived where Minnesota, Iowa, and South Dakota now meet.

* The seven tribes of the **Teton** or **Lakota Sioux** lived farther north and west.

* The **Santee** (san-TEE) or **Dakota Sioux** (da-KO-tah) lived near the Mississippi.

Clark Draws His Sword!

September 25, 1804 (Day 135)

Tensions mounted from the start of the Corps' encounter with the Teton Sioux. Without Pierre Dorian, who had stayed with the Yanktons, Clark noted, "we feel much at a loss for the want of an interpeter." (Neither Drouillard nor Cruzatte understood Sioux.) It also didn't help that three Teton leaders were struggling with each other for more power. On one visit to the keelboat, the leaders, including Untongarabar (Black Buffalo) and Tortohongar (the Partisan), became "troublesome." The captains had to force them to leave in a pirogue. When it reached shore, three of Partisan's warriors grabbed its rope. Then Partisan pushed Clark, who drew his sword. On the keelboat, the men loaded the guns.

If anyone had fired a gun or shot an arrow at that moment, the Lewis and Clark expedition might have ended there. Did Lewis or Clark stop the crisis? No. Black Buffalo did. When the Corps pushed off two days later, both sides were still shouting threats at each other. Clark later described the Tetons as "the pirates of the Missouri." Not being able to establish friendly relations with the Tetons was one of Lewis and Clark's few failures.

WINTER AMONG THE MANDANS

October 24, 1804 (Day 164)

Violent winds, heavy snowfall, and freezing temperatures mark the long winters of the northern plains. Anxious to reach the Mandan villages before these harsh conditions set in, Lewis and Clark pushed the expedition north past what is now Bismarck, North Dakota. On October 24, they met their first Mandans.

Sheheke Shoat (White Coyote) and Posecopsahe (Black Cat), two Mandan leaders, welcomed the Corps and the Arikara (ah-RICK-ah-rah) leader who had traveled with them. "Our wish is to be at peace with all," Sheheke Shoat (sheh-HEH-kay shoat) told the captains. "If we eat, you shall eat; if we starve, you must starve also."

A week later, the Corps began building Fort Mandan across the river from the first Mandan village. The fort, according to Clark's measurements, was 1,606 miles (2,584 km) from Camp Wood. "The huts were in two rows, containing four rooms each, and joined at one end forming an angle," reported carpenter Patrick Gass. "The roofs were made shed-fashion [sloped to let snow slide off], making the outer walls about 18 feet (5.4 m) high."

ENGRAVING BY KARL BODMER, *MIH-TUTTA-HANGKUSCH, A MANDAN VILLAGE*, WHICH SHOWS MANDAN WOMEN WITH BULLBOATS

Was Peace Among Tribes Possible?

Lewis and Clark not only wanted to establish peace between the United States and the American Indians, but also among the various Indian tribes themselves to make trade safer. But that proved to be very difficult. Relationships between tribes were complicated, and the captains did not fully understand them. The Indians in this area fought over control of guns and control of trade along the upper Missouri. Some tribes, like the Mandan and Arikara, had long-standing rivalries. Mandan leader Black Cat said peace would "not only give him Satisfaction, but all his people." But another Mandan leader called the Arikaras "liers and bad men" and insisted that they always started the wars, causing the Mandans to fight back for protection and revenge. Even two Mandan leaders couldn't agree!

As for the Hidatsas (hih-DAT-sahs), allies and trading partners of the Mandans who lived just north of them, they often raided western tribes like the Shoshone (sho-SHO-nee), who lived in the foothills of the Rocky Mountains, to take their people and capture their horses (very valuable for trade). Despite the captains' pleas not to, Le Borgne (One Eye), a Hidatsa leader, still planned on attacking the Shoshones in the spring. Raids were one way young men proved themselves to be great warriors.

GOSH, CAN'T YOU GUYS JUST GET ALONG?

LIKE THE COLONISTS AND THE BRITISH?

POINT TAKEN.

Life in a Mandan Village

During the winter months at Fort Mandan, the Corps members and the Indians hunted buffalo and elk together, visited back and forth, and attended each other's ceremonies. The Indians were as curious about the Corps as the Corps was about them. The Mandans called Lewis "Long Knife" and Clark "Red Hair." They called Sheheke Shoat "Big White." Both captains thought highly of the Mandans and their culture.

Mandan society was centered around the village, which had two chiefs, one for peace and one for war. The two villages were built on bluffs to protect them from the Missouri River's floods. Each village consisted of groups of dome-shaped earth lodges surrounding a *plaza*, or central flat area. Scary-looking figures, representing sacred powers, and scalps taken by warriors hung from poles. Around each village was a wooden fence and beyond it were burial grounds marked by a ceremonial circle of skulls and burial scaffolds.

Mandan women built and owned the lodges, a concept new to white people. When a man married, he brought his clothes, weapons, and horses to his wife's lodge. Women also owned the gardening tools and farmed the fertile land below the village. They did all of the work around the lodge, cooking, cleaning, and caring for the children. The men spent their time hunting and raiding. Everyone wore buckskin clothes and moccasins decorated with porcupine quills. Men and women often painted their faces or hair with red dye. The Mandans used *bullboats* (pages 98–99) for travel along the Missouri.

Home, Sweet Home

From the outside, earth lodges look like igloos made of branches, grass, and dirt. Underneath is a large, sturdy structure made of wood. To build one, the Mandans dug a big, shallow circle. In the middle of the circle, they built a square arrangement of four tall posts and beams to support the roof. They stood 12 to 16 posts around the circumference and laid beams from one post to the next. Roof poles were laid from the outside to the inside beams. Then they leaned poles from the ground to the outside beams. Posts were also used to make a long entrance.

Next, the Mandans covered the structure with willow branches (leaving a smoke hole) and then covered the branches with grass and a thick layer of clay. The clay insulated the lodge, keeping it warm in the winter and cool in the summer. Finally, a buffalo skin was draped over the entrance.

TRY IT!

Tour the inside of an earth lodge at < **www. nps.gov/knri/lodge/ lodge_2.htm** >.

MAKE A MANDAN EARTH LODGE

Mandan kids made small versions of earth lodges. You can, too — indoors or out! It can be any size, as long as the center posts are two to three times taller than the outer posts and the circle's diameter is two to three times the height of the center posts. (For example, if your center posts are 8"/20 cm, your outer posts will be about 4"/10 cm, and the circle's diameter will be 16" to 24"/40 to 60 cm). For an indoor version, use foam board or cardboard for the ground and craft sticks and toothpicks for posts and beams. Break sticks or tape two together to get the lengths you need.

Supplies

➤ **Indoors:** cardboard (for a base), pencil, craft sticks, toothpicks, clay, grass
➤ **Outdoors:** trowel, bamboo garden stakes, twigs, grass, mud
➤ Glue, tape, or string
➤ Scissors
➤ Brown felt or paper

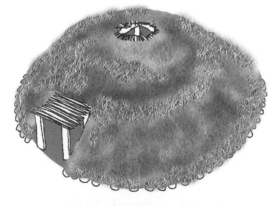

❶ **Indoors:** Draw a circle on the cardboard.
Outdoors: Dig a shallow circular hole in the ground.

❷ Use craft sticks or bamboo stakes and twigs as posts and beams to build a square structure in the center of the circle.

❸ Place 12 to 16 posts around the circumference of the circle.
Indoors: Glue or tape them in place.
Outdoors: Stick them in the dirt.

❹ Glue, tape, or tie beams from one post to the next. Lean poles from the cardboard or the ground to these beams. Lay poles from the outside circle to the inside square structure. Glue, tape, or tie down as needed.

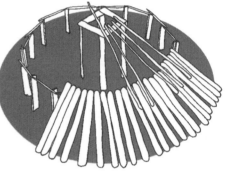

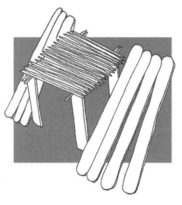

❺ Make a long entryway from beams and toothpicks or twigs. Cut brown felt (or paper) into the shape of a buffalo hide for a door.

❻ Cover the beams with a layer of twigs and grass and top with clay or mud.

Sheheke Shoat Draws a Map

Luckily for Lewis and Clark, the Mandans and Hidatsas knew the area to the west (today's Montana) from buffalo hunts and raids. Sheheke Shoat drew a map of the area in the dirt to show where the huge waterfall upriver was. The expedition would have to *portage* (carry on land) their boats and supplies around it. He made piles of sand for the great range of "shining mountains" they would have to cross and told the captains they could buy more horses from the Shoshones for the crossing.

TRY IT!

From memory, draw an outline of the United States in dirt like Sheheke Shoat did. Put in major rivers like the Mississippi and the Missouri, pile sand or rocks into mountain ranges such as the Appalachians and the Rockies, and make depressions for the Great Lakes and other large lakes. Now check a U.S. map. How did you do?

The Story of Sacagawea

November 4, 1804 (Day 175)

On November 4, Clark wrote that a French-Canadian fur trader named Toussaint Charbonneau (too-SAN shar-bo-NO), living among the Hidatsa, wanted to be hired as an interpreter. That was fine with the captains, who wanted to compile a vocabulary of Hidatsa words. The trader also had two young Shoshone wives. That really caught the captains' attention. If one of his wives came along, the expedition would have an interpreter for trading for horses with the Shoshone. Translating would be complicated but manageable: The wife could translate Shoshone into Hidatsa for Charbonneau, who could then speak to Drouillard in French, who would translate the French into English. Besides, the Shoshone wife might even remember landmarks near her home and help them to find her tribe!

The wife the captains chose was named Sacagawea (sa-CA-ga-WE-uh). About four years earlier, Hidatsa warriors had raided a band of Shoshones camped past the waterfall in an area where the Missouri divided into smaller rivers called Three Forks. Sacagawea was captured; her mother and several other Shoshones were killed. The name Sacagawea was probably given to the girl by the Hidatsa. Some time later Charbonneau apparently bought her and then took her as a wife. Now about 16, Sacagawea was soon to give birth to her first child.

Sacagawea or Sacajawea?

Sacagawea (sa-CA-ga-WE-uh) with a hard "g" sound, is Hidatsa for "Bird Woman." Sacajawea (SACK-ah-jah-we-ah), accented differently and with a "j" sound, sounds like a Shoshone word meaning "boat launcher." Which is right? No one knows for sure, but when Lewis named a creek after her on May 20, 1805, he wrote its name in his journal as "Sah ca gah we ah or bird woman's River."

Travel with the Corps

Winter on the Plains

The winter was "colder than I ever [knew] it to be in the States," wrote Ordway. Gass reported on December 6 that "in the night the river froze over." Two days later, Clark noted, "The Thermometer Stood at 12 degrees below 0." The temperature kept falling, to 21 below, then to 45 below zero. Ordway reported that it was so cold "the Sentinel [soldier on watch] had to be relieved every half hour." On January 10th, a Mandan "boy, about 13 years of age, Came to the fort with his feet frosed," Clark wrote. The boy had been lost overnight and had "only a Buffalow Robe to Cover him." The captains soaked the boy's frozen toes in cold water, the standard treatment for frostbite at that time. Two weeks later Lewis had to amputate the toes of one of the boy's feet and five days later the toes of the other.

How quickly it turned cold seems to have surprised the captains. They failed to bring the boats out of the river in time. "The situation of our boat and perogues is now allarming," wrote Lewis on February 3. "They are firmly inclosed in the Ice and almost covered with snow. We then determined to attempt freeing them from the ice by means of boiling water." When that failed, they tried chipping them out with axes and iron spikes. Finally, on February 26, the men got the boats up on land for needed repairs.

Travel with the Corps

February 11, 1805 (Day 274)

Lewis certainly didn't expect his next bit of doctoring. On February 11, he helped Sacagawea deliver her baby! Her labor was long and painful, so a French trader who lived with the Mandans suggested giving her a bit of the crushed rattle of a rattlesnake. He said it could speed up a baby's birth. Lewis had some rattles among his collections, so he crushed one in water for Sacagawea to drink. Ten minutes later she gave birth to a baby boy who was named Jean Baptiste (jaun bap-TEEST). Later, Clark would nickname him "Pomp" or "Pompey."

Dear Mr. President ...

While men hunted and the blacksmiths John Shields and Alexander Willard made *battle-axes* (large axes with broad blades used as weapons) to trade for corn, Sergeant Gass supervised the making of six dugout canoes to replace the keelboat. The captains prepared materials and packed boxes to send back to Jefferson. Clark drew maps both from his and Lewis's notes from the trip upriver and from information they learned from Indians and traders over the winter. His map of the part of the Missouri they had traveled was the most accurate that had been drawn to date. Lewis wrote many reports, including ones on Mandan horsemanship and the prospects for trade.

In the boxes were antelope skins, coyote bones, elk horns, Mandan corn, bows and arrows, 67 samples of soil and minerals, and 60 plants. There were cages with four live *magpies* (noisy, colorful birds related to bluejays), one live prairie dog, and a live grouse. A large trunk contained a buffalo robe painted by a Mandan man that showed a battle where Arikaras and Teton Sioux fought the Mandans and Hidatsas. (This robe is now in a museum at Harvard University.)

Meanwhile, Back at the White House

In the fall of 1804, while Lewis and Clark were with the Mandans, Jefferson was re-elected president. In the summer, he had met with Osage (OH-sage) tribal leaders from St. Louis whose visit Lewis had arranged before he left Camp Wood. Jefferson had heard from a trader in the fall that the expedition had made it to the Platte River (page 47). That was all the president knew about the expedition.

There was still some opposition to the Louisiana Purchase, so Jefferson defended it in his second inaugural address. "Is it not better that the opposite bank of the Mississippi should be settled by our brethren [members of the same society, meaning fellow Americans] and children, than by strangers from another family [the French and Spanish]?" he asked. "With which shall we be most likely to live in harmony?"

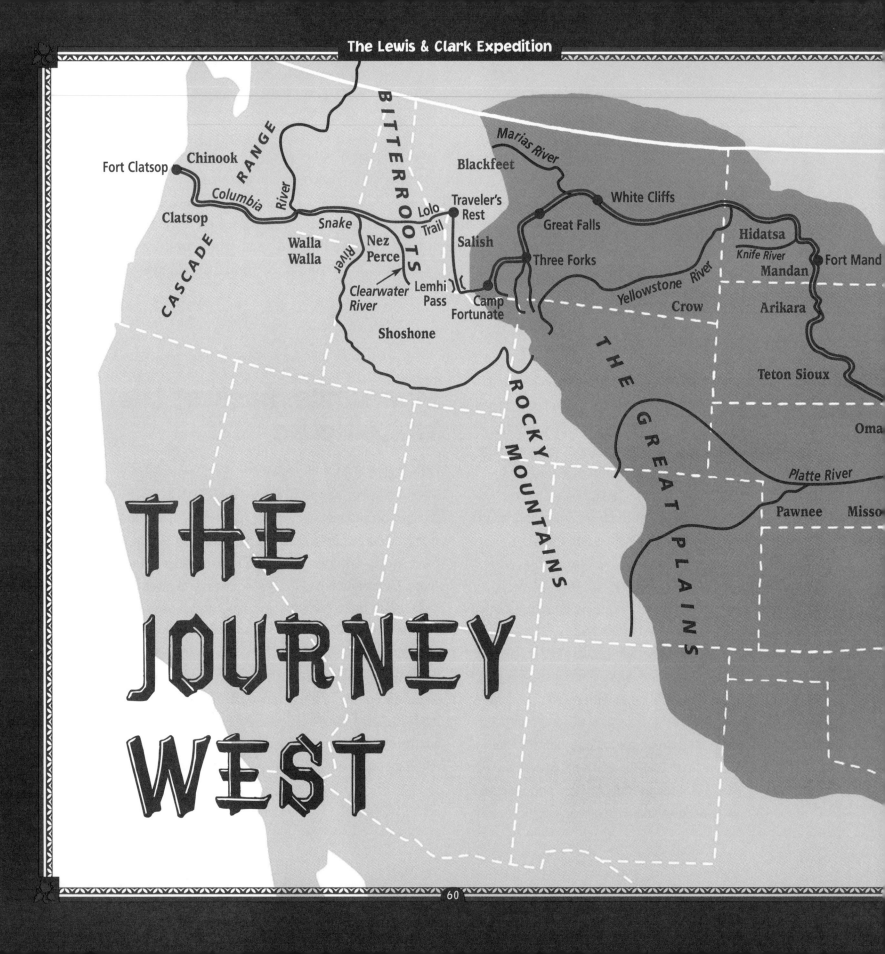

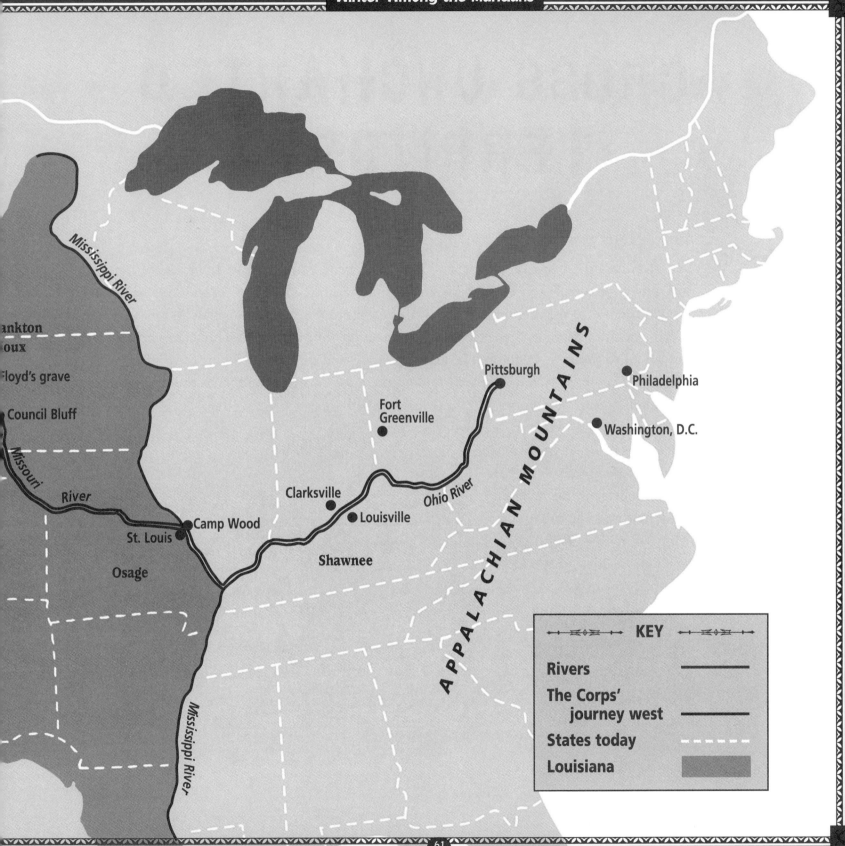

Mississippi River

ankton
oux

Floyd's grave

Council Bluff

Missouri

River

St. Louis

Osage

Camp Wood

Clarksville

Louisville

Shawnee

Mississippi River

Fort
Greenville

Pittsburgh

Philadelphia

Washington, D.C.

Ohio River

APPALACHIAN MOUNTAINS

KEY

Rivers

The Corps'
journey west

States today

Louisiana

ACROSS UNCHARTED TERRITORY

Travel with the Corps

April 7, 1805 (Day 329)

"We dismissed the barge [keelboat] and crew with orders to return without loss of time to St. Louis. Our vessels consisted of six small canoes and two large perogues. This little fleet, altho' not quite so rispectable as those of Columbus or Capt. Cook, were still viewed by us with as much pleasure as those deservedly famed adventurers ever beheld theirs ... We were now about to penetrate a country at least two thousand miles [3,218 km] in width, on which the foot of civilized man had never trodden; the good or evil it had in store for us was for experiment yet to determine, and these little vessells contained every article by which we were to expect to subsist [keep themselves alive] or defend ourselves ... I could but esteem this moment of my departure as among the most happy of my life. The party are in excellent health and sperits ... and anxious to proceed; not a whisper of murmur or discontent to be heard among them, but all act in unison, and with the most perfect harmony."

—*Captain Meriwether Lewis, in his journal*

Precious Cargo

The Permanent Party, including Sacagawea and her baby, now numbered 33. Their goal for this part of the journey was to get to Three Forks (page 57), find the Shoshones, and buy horses. The men, including York, had been forged into a team over the winter and now worked together like a well-oiled machine.

Without the clumsy keelboat, travel was faster, but it was also riskier. The Missouri's current was still against them and so was the wind, which swept across the high plains, blowing sand and whipping up waves. The pirogues tipped over more easily than the heavy keelboat. The dugout canoes, with their rounded bottoms, were even less safe.

Lewis and Clark packed the most precious cargo — instruments, journals, and Indian gifts — in the white pirogue, which was the steadiest boat. One of the captains usually rode in it, along with Drouillard, Charbonneau, and Sacagawea, with Pomp bundled on her back. Six soldiers, including the three who didn't know how to swim, paddled the craft.

The Sleeping Tepee

Lewis was so fascinated by the Sioux tepees that he bought one at Fort Mandan. It's likely that Sacagawea put the tepee up each night and took it down in the morning, probably with help from York. The tepee served as sleeping quarters for Lewis, Clark, Drouillard, Charbonneau, Sacagawea, and Pomp. Their beds were buffalo skins and wool blankets. The other men slept on buffalo robes under the stars.

CARVE A CANOE

The Indians made dugouts from tree trunks. After they removed the bark, they leveled one side of the log for the top of the canoe. Then the bottom was smoothed and rounded and the ends shaped. Hollowing out the log was hard work.

The Corps left its dugouts plain, but you can decorate yours. How about painting a sun or a buffalo on the sides? Then test your canoe in a tub of water. Does it bob like a cork or sink like Lewis's collapsible canoe (page 16)?

Note: Please ask adult permission to fill a tub, kiddie pool, or deep basin with water. And remember: Even a few inches (cm) of water can be very dangerous to infants and toddlers. If little children are around, you will need an adult to supervise. Thank you.

Supplies

- ➜ Old newspaper
- ➜ Large cake pan
- ➜ 2" x 2" x 12" (5 x 5 x 30 cm) block of balsa wood (from a craft or hobby store)
- ➜ Paring or utility knife
- ➜ Chisel or screwdriver
- ➜ File or sandpaper

Note: Ask an adult for permission to use the knife and other tools and for help with using them (especially the utility knife, which is *very* sharp). Always cut downward and away from your body.

❶ Place the pan on a thick layer of newspaper (to protect your work surface and collect the wood shavings). Stand the block in the pan.

❷ Use the knife to whittle away the two square edges along one side. Keep turning the block end to end to work along the entire length.

❸ Lay the block on its remaining flat side (the top) to carve and shape the ends. Make one end pointed for the bow and the other blunt for the stern.

❹ On the top surface, draw the inside shape of a canoe about ½" (1 cm) in from the edges. Cut along this outline and in a crisscross pattern inside it.

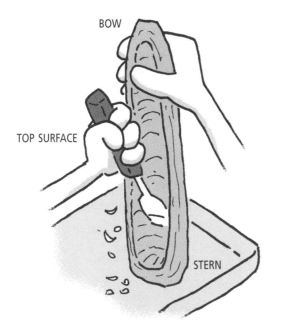

BOW

TOP SURFACE

STERN

Continue until the bottom is rounded and the sides are slightly curved as shown.

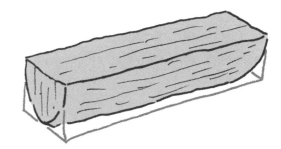

SIDE VIEW (BOAT UPSIDE DOWN)

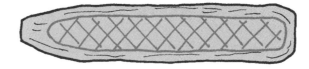

Chip away the wood with the point of the knife or the chisel to hollow out the inside. When you've finished, check the shape of the bow and stern and smooth any sharp edges with the file.

THE SHARP-BLADED *ADZE* WAS ONE OF THE TOOLS USED TO MAKE DUGOUTS.

Howling Hunters

Every day the journal writers mentioned huge herds of buffalo, elk, deer, and pronghorn antelope feeding on what looked to Lewis like "one common and boundless pasture." The hunters killed only what the Corps needed for food. That was plenty enough. Hungry from hard work, each man ate as much as 10 pounds (4.5 kg) of meat a day!

The men weren't the only hunters on the plains. Lewis observed that packs of gray wolves would run after a buffalo until it was exhausted and encircle a sick or injured one. Lewis noted that although the gray wolf was smaller than the eastern wolf and didn't burrow, it did howl. Imagine hearing *that* out in the wilderness at night!

Staying Healthy on the Trail

Sacagawea hunted for a different kind of food. She dug up wild roots, including Jerusalem artichokes, a type of sunflower with an edible *tuber* (an underground portion that looks like a potato), and prairie turnips (another potato-like tuber). She picked berries and wild licorice (the sweet roots were eaten directly or used for flavoring). Lewis noted that her efforts made the diet healthier. Still, the men were often sick with diarrhea, fevers, and other troubles. Lewis doctored everyone as usual. Even Seaman needed his attention when a beaver badly bit one of his hind legs.

The most common complaint was sore eyes. Sun and sand were constantly in their eyes. "So penitrating is this sand," complained Lewis, "that we cannot keep any article free from it; in short we are compelled to eat, drink, and breath it." Following Dr. Rush's instructions, he mixed two of his medicines to make a wash to soothe sore eyes.

➤ TRY IT! ➤

Sample one of the vegetables that Sacagawea gathered on the trail. Check the produce department at the grocery store for Jerusalem artichokes (sometimes called sunchokes). You can steam, boil, or bake them just like potatoes. High in iron and low in fat, they're very nutritious!

The Yellowstone River

The Hidatsas had told the captains about a large tributary of the Missouri that "waters one of the fairest portions of Louisiana, a country not yet hunted, and abounding in animals of the fur kind." They said the canoes could take it to the foothills of the Rocky Mountains and then continue overland to Three Forks.

April 25, 1805 (Day 347)
1,885 miles (3,033 km) from Camp Wood

That morning, Lewis set off overland with Joseph Field, three others, and Seaman to find the Yellowstone. The Hidatsa were right. A few hours later, Lewis came upon a country "covered with herds of Buffaloe, Elk & Antelopes, so gentle that we pass near them while feeding, without appearing to excite any alarm in them."

The next morning, after sending Field to explore the Yellowstone, Lewis took latitude and longitude measurements and examined the region. Eagles and magpies nested in the trees. In the low areas were bushes and trees loaded with berries, chokecherries, and purple currants. The air was filled with the scent of honeysuckle.

Then the whole party met where the two rivers joined. According to Clark, the Missouri was 330 yards (297 m) wide and very deep there, while the Yellowstone was almost as wide but much more shallow. Field reported that it had many sandbars and a gentle current. The captains never thought to follow the Hidatsa advice and switch to the Yellowstone, however. Following Jefferson's orders, they continued on the Missouri. After dinner, the men danced to Cruzatte's fiddle to celebrate reaching their first landmark since Fort Mandan, 278 miles (447 km) behind them.

Travel with the Corps

Hunting for Grizzlies

"The Indians give a very formidable account of the strength and ferocity of this anamal [the grizzly bear]," reported Lewis. After killing one on April 29, he boasted, "The Indians may well fear this anamal equiped as they generally are with their bows and arrows, but in the hands of skillfull riflemen they [the bears] are by no means as formidable or dangerous as they have been represented." Lewis didn't boast for long.

On May 14, six men went out to kill a bear. Four men "fired nearly at the same time and put each his bullet through him," recounted Lewis. "In an instant this monster ran at them with open mouth."

"It chased 2 men in to a cannoe," reported Whitehouse. "They fired at him. Some of the men on Shore wounded him worse." The bear, continued Lewis, then "pursued two of them … so close that they were obliged to throw … themselves into the river altho' the bank was nearly twenty feet [6 m] perpendicular; so enraged was this anamal that he plunged into the river only a few feet behind." Just in time a man on shore "Shot the bear through the head, which killed him dead," wrote Whitehouse, who noted that "his nales [nails or claws] was Seven Inches [17.5 cm] long." A month later, it was Lewis's turn to run into the river to escape a grizzly, "open mouthed and full speed."

⊷⊶ TRY IT! ⊷⊶

It's likely that the men told stories of their narrow escapes from bears around the campfire at night, maybe even exaggerating the events in the telling. Have you ever had a narrow escape? Gather your friends or family, and by flashlight, tell your own "tall" tales. Be as outrageous as you like!

White Pirogue Almost Sinks!

While men were escaping the grizzly on shore, there was another near disaster, this one on the river. A sudden gust of wind turned the white pirogue around while it was under sail. Charbonneau, who was at the rudder controlling and directing the boat, panicked. He dropped the rudder, which caused the boat to tip onto its side. In an instant waves slopped over the side and light articles floated out.

Both captains were on shore nearly panicking themselves. They yelled and fired their rifles into the air to get the attention of the crew, but the sounds were drowned in the wind and hollering on the boat. Cruzatte was shouting at Charbonneau to get control of the rudder and turn the boat into the wind. But the interpreter wasn't listening. He was pleading with the Heavens for mercy, perhaps because he couldn't swim — or perhaps because Cruzatte took out his gun and threatened to shoot him if he didn't obey his orders!

Charbonneau finally took up the rudder, but it was too late. The boat was full of water. Back on shore Lewis thought about diving into the cold, rushing water to save his precious cargo, but the boat was 300 yards (270 m) away so he didn't. Luckily, Cruzatte again took charge, ordering two men to starting bailing and others to paddle. They finally got to shore.

What was Sacagawea doing with everyone around her panicking? With Pomp on her back, she calmly reached out and caught most of the articles that were washed overboard! Lewis noted her courage and presence of mind. "Some of the papers and nearly all of the books got wet," reported Whitehouse, "but not altogether Spoiled." After this near disaster, the captains started making two copies of all important reports.

"I beheld the Rocky Mountains for the first time."

May 26, 1805 (Day 378)

Toward the end of May, as the Corps pressed on toward Three Forks, it traveled across what's now northern Montana. The Missouri began twisting through rugged bluffs, and the land was "a desert, barren country," according to Lewis. The air was pure and dry. Clark thought the area would never be settled. He observed an animal with big horns that was "peculiar to this upper part of the Missouri." It was a bighorn sheep high in the cliffs that amazed everyone as it "bound from rock to rock," wrote Lewis. The captains also observed abandoned tepees and worn-out Indian moccasins. Sacagawea examined them; they weren't Shoshone.

On May 26 from the top of a bluff, Lewis wrote: "I beheld the Rocky Mountains for the first time." Capped with snow, the mountains glistened in the afternoon sun. The sight, despite its beauty, made Lewis worry about the "sufferings and hardships" his men would have to face in crossing the mountains. (Actually, the mountains Lewis saw this early were probably the Bearpaw Mountains in north-central Montana.)

The men were suffering enough as is. Rocks, rapids, and shallow water made paddling impossible. Day after day they walked in cold water, sometimes up to their armpits, tugging the boats along. "In short," wrote Lewis, "their labour is incredibly painfull and great, yet those faithfull fellows bear it without a murmur." Perhaps the scenery helped. Above them loomed beautiful rocky white cliffs worn by wind and water into fascinating shapes.* On May 31, Lewis wrote, the water "has trickled down the soft sand cliffs and woarn it into a thousand grotesque figures."

FROM THE CLIFFS ALONG THE MISSOURI RIVER IN MONTANA, LEWIS MISTAKENLY THOUGHT HE WAS VIEWING THE ROCKY MOUNTAINS, AS REFLECTED IN OLAF SELTZER'S PAINTING *LEWIS'S FIRST GLIMPSE OF THE ROCKIES*.

*Today, this section of the river is called the Missouri River Breaks and White Cliffs. One of the few places that remains as it was when Lewis and Clark passed through, it is now protected as a Wild and Scenic River (a preservation program managed by the National Park Service).

Decision at the Marias

June 3, 1805 (Day 386)

The Corps came upon an unexpected fork in the river. The river on the north side had thick, muddy water just like the river they had been on for so long. The river on the south side had clear water and a stony bed as rivers do when they come out of mountains. Which fork was the Missouri? If they took the wrong one, they could miss their chance to meet the Shoshones and get horses.

To decide, Clark set off overland to explore the southern river; Lewis explored the northern fork. They plotted the rivers' courses and observed new animals and plants. After several days, Lewis and Clark returned, convinced the southern fork had to be the Missouri. Their men disagreed.

In a remarkable act of respect, Lewis and Clark decided that Lewis, Drouillard, and three privates would hike ahead along the southern fork to find the waterfall the Indians had mentioned. If they did, great! If they didn't, they could hurry back to Clark and the others, who would follow more slowly on the river. That way, they wouldn't lose too much time if the captains were wrong. First they hid the red pirogue and buried some supplies to lighten the load. Lewis named the northern fork the Maria's (now spelled Marias) River after a cousin.

LEWIS'S JOURNAL ENTRY AND DRAWING OF THE HEATH COCK OR COCK OF THE PLAINS, ALSO KNOWN AS SAGE GROUSE

THINK ABOUT IT

Follow the Leader?

All the men disagreed with Lewis and Clark about which river was which, yet according to Lewis, "they said very cheerfully that they were ready to follow us any wher [where] we thought proper to direct." What do you think it is about the two captains that would allow the men to agree to follow them "cheerfully" even when they are convinced the leaders are wrong? Do you think all the work Lewis and Clark put into building a team paid off?

The Great Falls

June 13, 1805 (Day 396)

The captains had been right. Three days from the Marias, Lewis's "ears were saluted with the agreeable sound of a fall of water." He soon was gazing at "the grandest sight I ever beheld." He wrote about the water tumbling 80 feet (24 m) over a rocky ledge with "incredible swiftness" and "flying up in jets of sparkling foam" when it hit the rocks below. He used words like majestic, sublime (awe-inspiring because of great beauty), and grand, and said the sight filled him with "pleasure and astonishment."

The river here was full of fish unknown to science, including cutthroat trout and sauger (a type of perch), which Lewis took time to describe before eating some for dinner.

The next morning one man went back to tell Clark about the falls, while Lewis scouted ahead. He found a small waterfall at the end of the rapids of the first falls. Then Lewis heard "a tremendious roaring" and discovered another falls, then another and another. The Great Falls* wasn't a single waterfall (and a day's portage), as the Indians had described, it was more than *18 miles (29 km)* of five falls and rapids!

Despite the beauty around him and the warm summer weather, Lewis was in a hurry. He knew the Corps had to cross the mountains before winter, which came early to the Rockies.

⦿ TRY IT! ⦿

You can see how impressed Lewis was with the natural beauty of the falls by his choice of descriptive words. Instead of saying "We have reached a beautiful waterfall," he describes it as grand and majestic, even sublime. Can't you picture the foaming water rushing over the rocks (and almost feel the spray) from his description?

Think of an area of great natural beauty that you live near or have visited. Playing with words, use them as tools (just as you would a paintbrush and watercolors) to create visual images of the area and capture its beauty or the feelings it evokes.

*The city of Great Falls, Montana, settled in 1884, is named for this series of waterfalls. Several dams have been built on the river, the first one in 1891.

The Great Falls Portage

Clark scouted the portage route and measured the height of each falls. The total was nearly 363 feet (109 m). At their camp below the falls (called Lower Camp), Lewis directed the men in how to build two carts out of the only tree in the area. They would cart the canoes and cargo; the white pirogue, too big to portage, was hidden. Lewis also cared for Sacagawea, who had been seriously ill with a fever for several days. He treated her with mineral water from a nearby sulfur spring as well as with other remedies he had brought.

The portage began on June 22. For the next 12 days, Clark led most of the men back and forth carting supplies between Lower Camp and Upper Camp on White Bear Island above the falls. Hail fell so big it knocked men down. A flash flood nearly swept away Clark, Sacagawea, and little Pomp. Wheels and towropes broke. But the worst plague was under their feet. The ground was covered with prickly pear cactus, named for its long, sharp spines and its pear-shaped fruit. The spines pierced right through the men's moccasins and cut their feet. "Maney limping from the soreness of their feet," noted Clark, who once pulled 17 spines from his own foot! Seaman's paws, too, were raw. Each night they camped at the end of the falls with Lewis and the others, who were assembling Lewis's collapsible iron-frame canoe, the *Experiment.* The Corps had lugged it along to replace the pirogues, but it leaked badly, so they lost more time making dugout canoes. Finally, on July 15, the Corps was back on the

TRY IT!

Remember the Yellowstone? Trace the path of the Yellowstone River on the map on page 60. The Indians had been right about it. Had the captains followed it, they could have skipped the Great Falls and gotten to Three Forks sooner. Of course, they didn't know what a tough portage it would be.

MAKE MOCCASINS

Between prickly pear cactus, barbed seeds of needle grass, and sharp stones, Ordway reported, "one pair of good mockinsons will not last more than about 2 days" on the portage. Men began making their moccasins with double soles. Make a pair of moccasins for yourself, but don't step on any prickly pears!

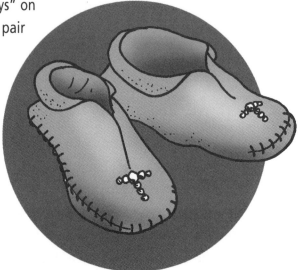

Supplies

- 2 large pieces of a paper grocery bag or other stiff paper, folded in half
- Ruler
- Pencil
- Craft scissors
- Leather, felt, or vinyl fabric, 12" x 15" (30 cm x 37.5 cm) per moccasin
- Fabric scissors
- Awl or hammer and nail
- Clothespin
- Yarn, leather cord, or rawhide
- Leatherwork needle or other strong sewing needle with a large eye
- Beads and glue (optional)

To make the pattern and cut out the leather:

❶ Place one foot on one piece of the folded paper so the instep (inner side) is about ½" (1 cm) from the fold. Holding the pencil vertically, trace around your foot. Label the pattern left or right.

❷ Your foot is three-dimensional, so for the moccasin to fit, you need to make the pattern longer and wider than your actual footprint. From the fold, draw a line that's ¾" (2 cm) larger than your traced footprint on all sides. Make the heel square.

❸ Cut out the paper pattern, being careful not to cut the fold. Open the pattern. Place it on the leather, felt, or vinyl and trace around it. Cut it out.

❹ Repeat steps 1 through 3 for the other foot.

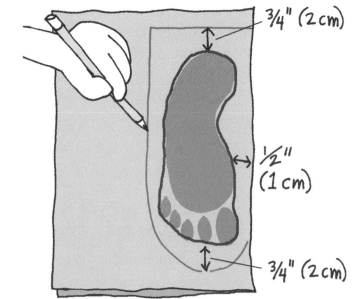

¾" (2 cm)

½" (1 cm)

¾" (2 cm)

To sew the moccasin:

❶ To make it easier to sew through the thick material, ask an adult to help you poke holes about ¾" (2 cm) apart for the stitches through both leather pieces as shown with an awl or a hammer and a nail.

❷ Fold the leather so the good side is out and stitch around the toe and down the side as shown, but not across the bottom.

❸ Cut a slit in the topside of the moccasin, parallel to the fold. The slit will be the opening for your foot.

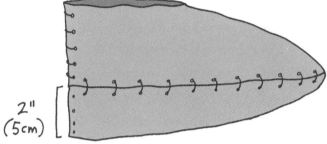

❹ Try on the moccasin to measure where to sew the heel. Pinch the heel closed with the clothespin; then, take off the moccasin and mark with pencil where the seam should be.

Cut off any excess leather and punch holes through both back pieces. Sew the back seam from the top to 2" (5 cm) from the bottom.

❺ About 1" (2.5 cm) from the bottom, cut a 1" (2.5 cm) slit as shown on both sides of the sole.

Sew the two flaps you just made to the bottom of the moccasin, punching any additional holes as necessary.

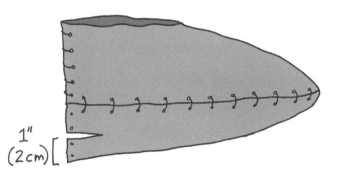

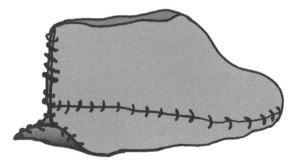

❻ To make a double-soled moccasin, trace around the finished shoe onto another piece of leather and cut just inside the line. Slip the insole into the moccasin. Repeat for the other shoe.

❼ Try on your moccasins. Enlarge the top opening if necessary. Fold down the top edge of the opening and sew or glue on decorative beads, if you like.

Gates of the Rocky Mountains

July 19, 1805 (Day 432)
2,712 miles (4,364 km) from Camp Wood

As the Missouri began to narrow and climb into the mountains, the Corps passed plains blazing with color from blooming prickly pears and sunflowers. Clark, York, Joseph Field, and John Potts went ahead by land to search for the Shoshones. On the river, Lewis complained, "we are almost suffocated in this confined vally with heat." That night the fleet entered a canyon with cliffs that rose 1,200 feet (360 m) straight up from the river's edge. Bighorn sheep climbed around on top. "Every object here wears a dark and gloomy aspect," wrote Lewis. He called the place "the gates of the rocky mountains."

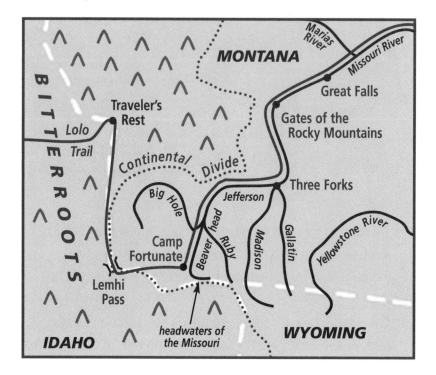

Three Forks

When Lewis met up with Clark beyond the "gates," Clark's news was as gloomy as the canyon. He had seen signs of Indians, but no Indians, and his feet were raw from prickly pears. But Sacagawea "cheered the sperits of the party," wrote Lewis, when she recognized the area as the "river on which her relations live, and that the three forks are at no great distance."

July 27, 1805 (Day 440)

On July 27, the mountains opened up into a beautiful bowl-shaped meadow ringed by lofty peaks. Two other rivers joined the one they were on. They had made it to Three Forks, but there were no Shoshones. Clark, exhausted and sick, rested. Lewis explored and measured latitude and longitude. The men repaired clothes and equipment. They were camped, Sacagawea told them, where she had been kidnapped.

August 8, 1805 (Day 452)

The captains decided to follow the fork on the right, naming it Jefferson's River (now called the Jefferson River). But it too forked into three branches — another time-consuming decision, another canoe accident. The men were now so fed up, they wanted to leave the boats and take to the land. Then Sacagawea pointed to a hill in the distance. Her people called it Beaver's Head and lived near it in the summer. The Corps followed the middle stream in that direction. Would they find the Shoshones there?

A Dream Dies

August 12, 1805 (Day 456)
More than 3,100 miles (4,988 km) from Camp Wood

Out searching for Shoshones with Drouillard, Shields, and Hugh McNeal, Lewis approached the *Continental Divide* (the spine of the Rockies that separates the areas that drain into the Atlantic Ocean on the eastern side from those that drain into the Pacific on the western side). McNeal "stood with a foot on each side of this little" stream that was the source for the Missouri and, reported Lewis, "thanked his god that he had lived to bestride the mighty & heretofore deemed endless Missouri."

His heart pounding with excitement, Lewis climbed through Lemhi Pass to the top of the Great Divide, just south of what's now Dillon, Montana. He expected to see the mountains slope down into another vast plain crossed by another mighty river that would lead them, finally, to the Pacific Ocean. Instead, he saw "immence ranges of high mountains still to the West of us." They were the Bitterroot Mountains, a rugged range at the beginning of the Rockies. The dream of an easy Northwest Passage died right at that moment. Was Lewis disappointed? Upset? Crushed? We don't know. He never wrote about it.

Delivery for President Jefferson

On the same day Lewis crossed the Continental Divide and left American soil for the first time, the boxes and cages sent from Fort Mandan arrived in Washington, D.C. As Jefferson read Lewis's optimistic reports and examined Clark's maps, he had no clue how difficult the journey really was or how high and rugged the western mountains were. He hung the elk antlers in the entrance to Monticello and planted the corn in his gardens, perhaps still dreaming of a Northwest Passage.

TRY IT!

If you have a vegetable garden, you can plant Mandan corn just as President Jefferson did. Mandan Bride and Mandan Red are two beautiful multicolored varieties that have been passed down from the Mandans in North Dakota (see Resources, page 107). Display the colorful ears or grind the kernels for a delicious "homegrown" cornbread! Then, dry the husks and make a cornhusk doll. You'll be helping to preserve an important part of Mandan culture.

Finding the Shoshones

The day before he crossed the Great Divide, Lewis had spied a Shoshone on horseback. As he, Drouillard, and the others approached, the Indian "suddonly turned his horse about, gave him the whip, leaped the creek and disapeared." The day after, the men came upon an old woman and two girls. The woman and younger girl cowered in fright until Lewis put down his gun, rolled up his sleeve to show the woman his white skin, and said "*tab-ba-bone*" (which Sacagawea had said meant "white man"). Convinced he wasn't an enemy Indian, she led the white men to her leader, Cameahwait (ca-ME-ah-wait), One Who Never Walks. He welcomed them to his village. The Shoshones shared berry cakes, the only food they had. Lewis gave the women and children mirrors, beads, and face paint.

Through Drouillard's signs, Lewis explained who they were and what they were doing. He told the leader that the rest of his party was at the river on the other side of the Great Divide. Would Cameahwait and his people go back with him and help carry the expedition's gear over the divide? Would the leader sell Lewis horses to cross the mountains and tell him what lay beyond? No plains, no buffalo for food, no navigable river, was the leader's disappointing answer.

As for horses and more help, Cameahwait said his people were hungry. It was time to ride east to Three Forks to hunt for buffalo. He complained that his people had no guns, although his enemies, the Blackfeet (a powerful tribe to the north) and Hidatsa, did. Lewis promised him the U.S. would trade guns with him if he helped the explorers. It was a promise Lewis knew couldn't be kept, but it worked. Cameahwait agreed to help.

◆━◁◆▷━◆ TRY IT! ◆━◁◆▷━◆

Lewis described a Shoshone hug and greeting that Cameahwait used. Put your left arm over the other person's right shoulder, touching his or her back, and place your left cheek on his or her right cheek. At the same time, say "ah-HI-eh, ah-HI-eh," which means "I am much pleased."

SIGN WITH THE SHOSHONE

Indian nations spoke different languages. When they met on hunting parties or to trade, they needed a way to communicate so they developed a common sign language. Many of the signs are easy to understand. They are like pictures drawn with your hands. Imitate the ones shown here. Can you tell what Lewis (through Drouillard, green) and Cameahwait (brown) are saying? See the answer below.

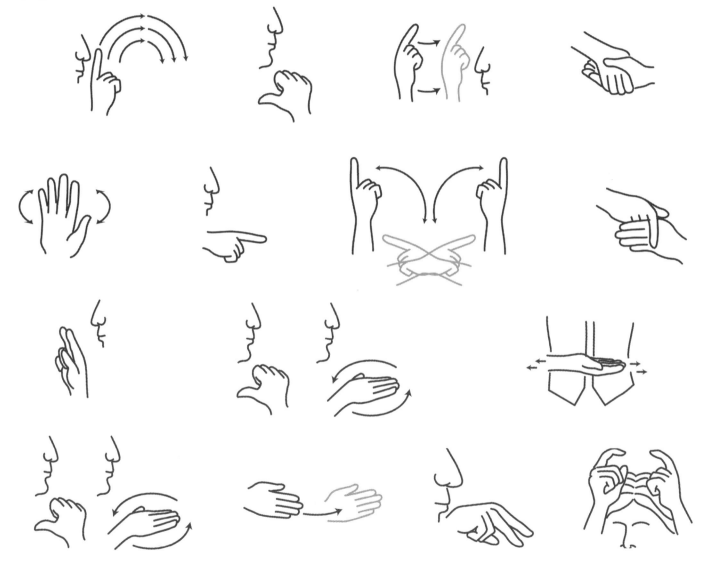

Answer:

(signs) Chief me come peace
(English) Chief, I come in peace.

question you trade horses
Will you trade horses?

(signs) friend me-all hungry
(English) Friend, we are hungry.

me-all go hunt buffalo
We go hunt buffalo.

A Surprise at Camp Fortunate

Despite their friendliness, Cameahwait and his people were suspicious of going with Lewis to meet Clark, who was still on the river east of the Great Divide. They had recently suffered an attack by the Blackfeet. Was this an ambush? Still, on August 16, a group of 28 Shoshone men and three women followed their leader and Lewis to the place the captains had agreed to meet. There was only one problem — Clark wasn't there! The Shoshones' suspicions grew.

The next morning, much to Lewis's relief, Clark arrived with Charbonneau and Sacagawea. Later, the canoes arrived and Camp Fortunate was established. The white men, York, and Seaman fascinated the Indians. They called the air gun (page 15) "great medicine." Then Lewis and Clark sat down with Cameahwait to negotiate a trade for horses, asking Sacagawea and Charbonneau to join them to interpret.

Call it luck, call it destiny, but what happened next was totally unbelievable. Sacagawea had been staring at the leader, when suddenly she "jumped up, ran & embraced him, & threw her blanket over him and cried." She recognized Cameahwait — he was her brother! Now, the captains thought, there was no question the Shoshones would help.

August 18, 1805 (Day 462)

Cameahwait told Lewis and Clark that the Nez Perce (nez PURSE) Indians lived on a river that "ran a great way toward the seting sun and finally lost itself in a great lake." That must be the Columbia, the captains figured, but how could they get to it? The river that led into it (the Salmon River, which crosses Idaho), answered Cameahwait, was impassable. The best route was to the north, overland through the Bitterroots, along a trail the Nez Perce used.

Still wanting to go by water, Clark and 11 men went ahead on August 18 to scout the river route. Meanwhile, Lewis and the others stayed at Camp Fortunate for six days, repacking their supplies for the overland route. Lewis traded a uniform coat, shirts and leggings, knives, and trinkets for nine horses and a mule. He wrote about the Shoshones, took measurements for latitude and longitude, and celebrated his 31st birthday.

On August 26, Lewis and his group traveled to a new camp at Lemhi Pass. John Colter was there with a message from Clark. Cameahwait was right. The river was "not navigable, no game and very mountaineous." They would need more horses for the overland trail. Suddenly, though, the price was higher. The Shoshones now demanded a rifle, pistol, and ammunition. In the end, the Corps bought 29 horses. Many of them were the poorest stock the Indians had. The Shoshones might be helpful, but they did have to look out for themselves first. They needed their best horses for the buffalo hunt.

A Betrayal?

Sacagawea overheard Cameahwait tell his warriors that they would leave on the buffalo hunt before the white men were ready to leave Camp Fortunate. When Lewis found out, he shamed the leader, saying he was betraying his promise to stay and help. Cameahwait told Lewis that he knew he had done wrong, but that his people were hungry.

Lewis realized that. He wrote about the Shoshones' poverty, mentioning their grass lodges, how thin Cameahwait was, and how "distressing" it was to see "poor starving children." Still, Lewis felt he had to hold the leader to his word. Without Shoshone help and horses, the expedition would fail. He did what he could, giving the Shoshones most of the 528 trout he caught in a willow net and several deer the hunters killed.

Anything Goes ... or Not!

Lewis and Clark's main concern is for the good of the Corps and for the expedition's success. As leader, Cameahwait's main concern is of course for his tribe and its critical need for a good buffalo hunt as well as for guns to defend itself. What do you think of Lewis's tactic of promising guns he knew he couldn't deliver? Or of Cameahwait's plan to leave Camp Fortunate before the Corps expected? Some would say that all is fair in the "game of survival," and that leadership involves doing whatever is necessary for your group's survival. Others might suggest that working together – with fairness – would make both groups stronger.

Take a stand on Lewis and Clark's and Cameahwait's tactics. Are you more sympathetic to one situation or the other, or do you feel that neither behavior was right?

OVER THE MOUNTAINS & TO THE SEA

September 1, 1805 (Day 476)

On September 1, the Corps set off north along the Continental Divide led by Old Toby, a Shoshone guide. The route was steep and rocky, and the weather was very cold. Three days later, in the Bitterroot Valley, they came upon 400 Salish (SAL-ish) Indians, who were on their way to join the Shoshones for the buffalo hunt. The Salish shared their berries and roots with the explorers, who traded for more horses. On September 9, the Corps came to the base of the Nez Perce trail (near Missoula, Montana). They named their camp Traveler's Rest and stayed for two days before heading over the mountains.

September 11, 1805 (Day 486)

On September 11, the Corps tackled what Gass called "the most terrible mountains I ever beheld." The Lolo Trail was a narrow 100-mile (161-km) footpath through thick pine and cedar forests. When Old Toby lost the main trail, the men hacked their way back through thickets. They climbed over rocky ridges, around fallen timber, and down deep ravines. Men and horses stumbled; some horses fell over the cliffs. The horse carrying Clark's desk rolled 40 yards (36 m) down a mountain. Unbelievably, the horse escaped injury, but the desk was smashed.

Finally, the Corps crawled back up to a ridge. At the higher elevation (where the air contains less oxygen), everyone gasped for breath. All they could see, wrote Clark on September 15, were "mountains in every direction."

September 17, 1805 (Day 492)

The weather — freezing rain and blinding snow — was even more challenging than the trail. But worst of all was the hunger. There was no game in the mountains. The men killed and devoured the colts. They finished off the portable soup. They ate a coyote. When there was nothing else, they ate candles. "I find myself growing weak for the want of food," wrote Lewis, 10 days after leaving Traveler's Rest.

On September 17, midway through the harrowing journey, Lewis and Clark decided that Clark and six hunters would hurry ahead to find game lower down and leave it for the others to eat. It was a tough decision to make. Clark's small group would be an easy target for any possible Indian attack on the prairie beyond the mountains. The Indians could then use their rifles to attack Lewis's group when they came down — if, that is, they got down before starving to death.

The Nez Perce to the Rescue

Clark's group did not find game on the prairie but they did find the Nez Perce, as Cameahwait had said. Their name comes from the French for pierced nose, yet nose piercing was not common among them. It seems that Drouillard may have misunderstood the sign the Shoshone used for them. Lewis and Clark called them Choppunish (chop-PUN-ish) or Nez Percé (nay pehr-SAY) in French. They called themselves — and still do — the Nimíipuu (nee-ME-poo), "people," and lived along the Clearwater, Snake, and Salmon rivers (in present-day Idaho), where they fished for salmon. Nez Perce hunters crossed the Bitterroots frequently to hunt buffalo. Clark and his group were the first white people to come to Nez Perce country.

On September 22, Lewis's group met one of Clark's men coming back with a horse carrying dried fish and camas roots from the Indians. They ate, hiked to the first Nez Perce village, and made camp. That night, Clark found Lewis and his party "weakened and much reduced in flesh as well as strength." They were also "much rejoiced to find something to eate." Clark warned them not to eat too much of the camas; he had already been sick from the roots, which caused gas and painful stomach cramps in people not used to them. Lewis and his men stuffed themselves anyway. Lewis was especially sick. Some of the men couldn't ride or work. Rush's Thunderbolts only made things worse.

EVEN WHEN DESPERATELY HUNGRY, LEWIS STILL OBSERVED WHAT WAS AROUND HIM. ONE OF THE BIRDS LEWIS DESCRIBED IN HIS JOURNAL IS STILL KNOWN TODAY AS LEWIS'S WOODPECKER, OR *MELANERPES LEWIS*. IT HAS GREENISH-BLACK WINGS, BACK, HEAD, AND TAIL, A RED FACE, LIGHT GRAY BREAST, AND A WHITE COLLAR AROUND ITS NECK.

A Woman Saves the Corps

The Nez Perce who met Clark's group were led by Walammottinin (Twisted Hair). According to tribal oral history (stories passed down by being told rather than written), some of his warriors wanted to kill the white men and take their goods. An old Nez Perce woman stopped them. Long ago she had been kidnapped by Blackfeet and taken into British North America where a white trader bought her. The whites she lived with had treated her well. Lewis and Clark were like them, she told the others. "Do them no hurt."

Twisted Hair agreed. He drew a map of the rivers that led to the Columbia on an elk skin. He led the men to a grove of ponderosa pines and showed them the Nez Perce way of using fire to hollow out logs to make five dugout canoes. He promised that his people would take care of the expedition's horses — now branded with "U.S., Capt. M. Lewis" — until the Corps returned. Twisted Hair even joined the expedition to help communicate with Indians downriver.

Travel with the Corps

Back on a River

October 7, 1805 (Day 512)

Nearly two months after leaving the Missouri, the Corps was once again on the water — the Clearwater River. If anyone thought that going downstream with the current was going to be easy, they quickly realized how wrong they were. The Clearwater and Snake (reached three days later) were mountain rivers with many rapids, "swifter," one man wrote, "than a horse could run." "One of the canoes Struck a rock in the middle of the rapid … cracked hir [her] So that it filled with water," wrote Ordway. "The waves roared over the rocks and Some of the men could not swim" but were rescued. The "canoe filed [filled] and Sunk," reported Clark. "Our loss of provisions is verry Considerable." Old Toby, the Shoshone guide, ran off. Running rapids was not for him.

October 16, 1805 (Day 521)

On October 16, the Corps reached the Columbia, "a very beautiful river," according to Gass. There they rested for a few days. Seven days later they were at Celilo Falls (now submerged by a dam at The Dalles, Washington) where, Clark wrote, they "let the canoes down by Strong ropes of Elk skin." Tortured by fleas, he continued, "every man of the party was obliged to Strip naked" to brush them off their bodies. The river rushed on "boiling & whorling in every direction" through canyons of black rock. It tumbled down narrow gorges in the Cascade mountains, but triumphed Clark, "We passed Safe to the astonishment of all the Indians … who viewed us from the top of the rock."

Life along the River

The country along the first part of the Columbia River was dry, with little game. The river was teeming with fish, however. Along the shores Indians fished and dried salmon on scaffolds. There was hardly any timber, making it difficult to find enough firewood. Once the men took some from Indians. They asked Twisted Hair for permission, but it wasn't really his to give.

These Indians were related to and spoke languages similar to the Nez Perce. Among them were Yakimas (YAK-eh-mas) and Walla Wallas (WA-la WA-las). Twisted Hair and Sacagawea's presence reassured them. Curious Indians piled into 18 canoes and followed the Corps downriver. The soldiers, who were sick of fish, bartered for dogs to eat. Lewis and Clark talked and smoked pipes with the leaders, and learned more about their customs. Clark described how Wishram (WIH-shram) Indians preserved dried salmon in long grass baskets.

Beyond the mountains, the river's banks suddenly sprang to life with lush, dense forests. The Indians from here to the coast were Chinook (shih-NOOK). Because the Nez Perce and the Chinooks were at war, Twisted Hair returned home. The Chinooks spoke a different language and lived in plank houses. They bound their ankles, which made their legs swollen, and pressed their babies' heads between two boards to flatten them. The Chinooks expected payment for going down their river and often took knives, axes, or blankets. To them, they were showing the Corps how important they were. To the Corps, it was stealing.

Lewis and Clark envied only one thing about the Chinooks — their cedar canoes. They were lightweight, wide in the middle, tapered at the ends, and had carved figures at the bow and stern. Lewis bought one in exchange for a dugout, a hatchet, and trinkets.

"O! the joy!"

November 7, 1805 (Day 543)

Toward the end of October, the river started to rise and fall like an ocean tide. The water tasted salty. Seagulls flew overhead and seals played in the current. Some Indians sported sailor clothes and spoke a few English words. These were all signs that the Pacific was near. On November 7, after the morning fog lifted, Clark looked up. "Ocian in view!" he underlined in his journal. "O! the joy!" There was "great joy in camp" as they listened to the "noise made by the waves brakeing on the rockey Shores."

CLARK'S FAMOUS JOURNAL ENTRY

"The Wife of Shabano [Charbonneau] our interpreter We find reconsiles all the Indians, as to our friendly intentions. A woman with a party of men is a token of peace."

—*Captain William Clark, in his journal, October 13, 1805*

On the Pacific

November 16, 1805 (Day 552)
4,162 miles (6,697 km)

The "great joy in camp" didn't last long. What the men thought was the ocean was just the widening of the Columbia into its large estuary (where a river's current meets the sea's tide). Seasick from the rolling waves, their clothes rotting in the damp air, they camped on the north shore of the estuary where rain, wind, and giant waves penned them in for six days. "I can neither get out to hunt, return to a better Situation, or proceed on," complained Clark.

Fortunately, Colter, Willard, and Shannon found a sandy beach with abandoned Chinook huts farther up the north shore, which made a more comfortable camp. Unfortunately, their rifles were stolen by Chinooks who lived nearby. Lewis got the rifles back. Clark threatened to shoot any Indian who stole from them. A friendlier, more helpful group of Chinooks, the Clatsop (CLAT-sop), lived on the south bank.

On November 16, at the new camp, Clark added up his latest distance estimates and recorded, "Ocian 4162 Miles [6,697 km] from the Mouth of <u>Missouri</u> R." First Lewis, then Clark searched for a site for a winter camp, mapped the estuary, and went along the ocean coast looking for trading ships. When they didn't see any, they named the point of land that curved around the northern tip of the estuary Cape Disappointment. Lewis carved his name on a tree there. Clark added his name and the words: "By Land from the U. States in 1804 & 1805."

Where to Winter?

By November 24, the Corps was running out of time to make a decision about where to build a winter fort. The choices were:

- Return inland where the weather is drier, you'd be near friendly Indians, and you'd have a headstart on the return journey.

- Stay near the ocean where you could make salt (page 88) to preserve meat for the return trip. If a ship sailed by, you could buy supplies and perhaps send a couple of men back East with copies of journals, reports, and maps.

If you stay near the ocean, you'd have to choose between staying at the present camp, which means you don't have to move again but you'll spend the winter near the unfriendly Chinooks, or moving to the south shore where the Clatsops live and there is more timber and larger game.

Lewis and Clark agreed the south shore was the best option. Still, in an extraordinary move, the captains decided to ask everyone's opinion. Even York and Sacagawea had a say. Clark tallied the vote in his journal.

The final tally: Both captains, York, and all the men except Shields voted to try to find a place on the south shore. Sacagawea agreed as long as there were edible roots to gather. A site on the south shore was found some miles (km) from the ocean. If the Corps hadn't found a suitable site, however, the captains would have faced another difficult decision because in that case, half the voters voted to stay put and the other half wanted to go inland. No one, it seems, minded that York and Sacagawea had an equal say.

A Long, Wet Winter

Working in constant rain, the men spent the next three weeks building Fort Clatsop a few miles (km) from the shore. Surrounded by a fence, it had two rows of cabins with a parade ground in the middle. It was almost ready by Christmas Day. The holiday dinner wasn't much — some spoiled elk meat, stale dried fish, a few roots, and only water to drink (the whiskey was long gone). Still the men sang and gave each other gifts — moccasins and baskets they had made, handkerchiefs, and twists of tobacco. Sacagawea gave Clark 24 white weasel tails.

RECONSTRUCTION AT FORT CLATSOP NATIONAL MEMORIAL

Over the winter, Lewis worked on his journals as well as descriptions of plants, animals, and local Indian tribes. Clark corrected and refined his maps. His new map included the tributaries of the upper Missouri and showed the Rockies as a wide range of mountains much higher than those in the East. He drew in the Cascade Range and showed the path of the Columbia River through them. Both captains sketched fish, birds, and plants.

The men made candles and smoked the meat the hunters brought in to preserve it. Sacagawea and some of the men sewed clothes from elk hides. They made, Gass reported, 338 pairs of moccasins. (That should be enough to get through the prickly pears!) Another way of preserving meat required salt, so the expedition's salt-makers boiled seawater in large kettles on the beach day and night. As the water evaporated, the kettles became coated with salt. Their product was "excellent, fine, strong, & white," according to Lewis, who along with everyone except Clark, considered it a "great treat."

Mostly though, the Corps was cold, bored, and wet — on all but 12 days it rained. Often they were hungry and sick with a flu-like illness. It was a very different winter than the one they had spent with the Mandans.

TRY IT!

Mix ⅓ cup (75 ml) salt and 4 cups (1 L) water in a pan. With an adult's help, bring it to a boil. When you've boiled away all the liquid, scrape the salt out of the pan and spread it on a sheet of foil to dry. Compare the salt you "made" with the salt you began with. Does it taste the same, or is it more or less salty?

Indian Studies

During the winter, Lewis and Clark listed the different tribes and villages around the fort and estimated their populations. They described coastal Indian life and sketched hats, swords, and plank houses, as well as four different canoe styles and how they were made. The captains observed that the weather that kept the whites inside and grumbling was nothing to the Indians. Their skill at piloting their canoes allowed them to cross the choppy estuary, and their clothes protected them from the rain.

The Indians' capes shed water like rain slickers. Their cone-shaped hats, wrote Lewis, "are nearly waterproof, light, and I am convinced are much more durable than either chip [thin strips of wood] or straw." Made of cedar and a long, coarse grass, the hats had designs or pictures of men in canoes harpooning whales woven into them. Lewis and Clark had hats made for themselves and brought one back. With an eye toward future trade, Lewis learned that knives, fishhooks, kettles, and guns were in demand.

CLATSOP KNOB-TOP HAT

Jefferson Gets a Visit

January 4, 1806

On the other side of the continent, 45 leaders from 11 Indian nations visited President Jefferson, as was planned with the Yankton Sioux (page 51). In a long speech, Jefferson called Lewis "our beloved man" and thanked the Indians for helping him. He told them the United States population was growing and he wanted to see peace and trade between Indians and Americans. The leaders' reply was just as long. They agreed friendship and peace were good. They said they wished the "beloved man" well and had "him in our hearts." But they also complained that many of Jefferson's own people did not listen to him. "Tell your white Children on our lands, to follow your orders."

HOMEWARD BOUND

During the nearly three months at Fort Clatsop, Lewis and Clark had discussed the "homeward bound journey." They would start by heading back up the Columbia River to the Nez Perce village led by Twisted Hair (page 84), where they would collect their horses to cross the Bitterroots. It would be important to get there before the Indians left for the buffalo hunt in early summer. At Traveler's Rest on the other side of the Bitterroots, they talked about splitting up to explore more of the Louisiana Territory.

Lewis would lead a party northeast on horseback to check out a shortcut over the Continental Divide to the Great Falls that Old Toby had described. From there, he would explore the Marias River (page 71). Clark's party would head southeast to cross the divide and get to Three Forks, where they would pick up the Yellowstone. After both groups met where that river joined the Missouri, they would continue to the Mandan villages and then head down the Missouri to St. Louis before winter set in, they hoped. The two routes would allow them to pick up the pirogues, canoes, and other supplies they had hidden or buried along the way.

"The rain Seased [ceased] and it became fair about Meridien [noon], at which time we loaded our Canoes & at 1 P.M. left Fort Clatsop on our homeward bound journey."

—*Captain William Clark, in his journal, March 23, 1806*

The Corps Steals a Canoe

Lewis figured the expedition would need two more Indian canoes to get up the Columbia. He paid for one with his uniform coat but could not afford another. Desperate, he ordered several men to steal one from Coboway (cob-OH-way), the leader of the closest Clatsop village. It was the second time the expedition stole from Indians (remember the firewood?) and it was in direct violation of its own code of honor. Lewis tried to justify his behavior. During the winter several Clatsop men had stolen six elk from Drouillard. When the captains complained, Coboway paid them three dogs. Case closed. Right? Apparently not to Lewis, who used that theft to excuse his own.

According to Ordway, Lewis admitted it "set [felt] a little awkward." It must have. Coboway had been one of the few Chinooks who had been helpful. Perhaps in an effort to make amends, Lewis turned Fort Clatsop over to him. On a wall in the fort, he had tacked a list of the names of the men and a sketch of Clark's map.

THINK ABOUT IT

"They weren't our friends anyway"

Lewis would never have thought of stealing a canoe from the Mandans, but the Chinooks and Clatsops were a different story. They had never become the captains' friends. There were few social visits and no celebrations with one another at Christmas or New Year's. Communication was also more difficult because no one on the expedition spoke the Chinook language.

All in all, the captains disliked and distrusted these Indians for superficial reasons, including their appearance and even the sound of their language! With the bad weather, the isolation, and their general dislike of them, the captains and their men were angry, annoyed, and more than willing to behave badly to get another canoe, which they desperately needed. Does the Corps' situation justify its behavior?

To the Nez Perce

April 1, 1806 (Day 688)

Lewis and Clark had planned on eating fish on the Columbia, but Chinooks coming down the river told them the Indians upriver were starving because the salmon were not running yet. (In the spring, when the salmon swim upstream in large numbers to lay their eggs, it's called the *salmon run*.) The Corps couldn't wait for the salmon; they'd risk missing the Nez Perce. So the expedition stopped to prepare deer and elk jerky. Then they proceeded on, struggling against rapids, waves, wind, and rain, and making difficult portages.

April 11, 1806 (Day 698)

When the Corps reached the Cascades on April 11, tempers were running high again. For days, the men had been pestered by Chinooks. These river Indians were, Lewis believed, "the greatest theives and scoundrels we have met." One stole an ax and two threatened Shields. Three others stole Seaman — and that got Lewis good and mad. He sent three Corps members after them, and they brought Seaman back safe and sound.

With all these problems, the captains decided to leave the river, trade for horses, and march overland to the Nez Perce. But before they even started, they realized an Indian had taken a saddle. Lewis swore he would burn the man's village if it wasn't returned. Luckily it was, or Lewis might have done something that could have resulted in terrible consequences for his men as well as many innocent Indians. Lewis *did* burn the expedition's canoes so the river tribes couldn't use them.

April 27, 1806 (Day 714)

Soon the Corps was back with the Walla Wallas (page 85). What a difference! These Indians gave them fish and firewood. They returned knives and a steel hunting trap the soldiers had lost or left behind. The Corps had a big party with people from tribes of the area. Cruzatte played the fiddle and everyone sang and danced.

On April 30, the Corps headed for the Nez Perce via a shortcut that the captains had learned about from a Walla Walla leader. After a four-day march through snow and hail, they met up with a Nez Perce hunting party headed by a leader they knew.

Waiting with the Nez Perce

May 7, 1806 (Day 724)

The Bitterroots, Lewis wrote on May 7, "were in view. The Indians inform us that the snow is yet so deep on the mountains that we shall not be able to pass them untill the next full moon or about the first of June." Bad news, but the captains didn't waste the month. They talked peace and trade with Twisted Hair and other Nez Perce leaders. While Clark doctored, Lewis collected, described, and preserved several birds and almost 50 plants.

Lewis also studied and described Nez Perce clothing, personality ("cheerfull but not gay"), games, and horsemanship. He estimated there to be 4,000 Nez Perce in that area. Many individuals owned 50, 60, or 100 horses, mostly white, spotted Appaloosas. The captains arranged shooting matches, games, and horse races between their soldiers and Indian braves. Every day the Indians told them to wait a little longer before traveling on — the mountains were still covered in snow.

Doctoring for Horses

The price of horses was steep. Lewis had to part with two large kettles for four horses. That left only four small kettles for the expedition's cooks. Another horse cost him his dueling pistol; another, Clark's sword and some ammunition. Among the Nez Perce and tribes related to them, the captains took advantage of Clark's newfound fame as a doctor.

The year before, Clark had rubbed *liniment* (medicated ointment) on the knee of an old man who couldn't walk. He recovered. Now other sick Indians — sometimes 50 at a time — wanted to trade horses and food for Clark's doctoring skills. It was a good deal for both sides. The Indians got better and the Corps eventually left for the Bitterroots with 65 horses, including some fat young colts, which could be eaten if necessary.

Travel with the Corps

Back over the Bitterroots

June 14, 1806 (Day 762)

Running out of patience, Lewis and Clark decided to tackle the Lolo Trail over the Bitterroots against Indian advice and without Indian guides. "From hence to traveller's rest," Lewis wrote on June 14, "we shall make a forsed [forced] march." But both captains were worried. Wrote Clark: "I Shudder with the expectation with [of] great dificuelties ... from the Debth [depth] of Snow and the want of grass Sufficient to Subsist our horses."

They were right to worry. On the third day they were enveloped "in snow from 12 to 15 feet [3.6 to 4.5 m] deep." Lewis continued: "If we proceeded and should get bewildered in these mountains the certainty was that we should loose [lose] all our horses and consequently our baggage, instruments, perhaps our papers ... we conceived it madnes to proceed without a guide."

The Corps, reported Gass, "turned back melancholy and disappointed." The next day, he wrote, "two men went on ahead to the [Nez Perce] village to enquire for a guide." The guides they hired, Lewis wrote on June 26, "led us over and along the Steep Sides of tremendious Mountains entirely covered with snow." They cost Lewis three rifles, but he noted a day later that without their assistance "I doubt much whether we ... could find our way to Travellers rest." This time crossing the Bitterroots took just six days.

Lewis's Route

Travel with the Corps

July 3, 1806 (Day 781)

From Traveler's Rest, Lewis, nine men, and 17 horses rode along the Blackfoot River. Their Nez Perce guides had left them, to avoid meeting enemy Indians. Lewis's group crossed the Continental Divide at a place now called the Lewis and Clark Pass and headed northeast to the Missouri. They were in Louisiana Territory again, back on plains filled with buffalo, elk, wolves, deer, and … grizzlies. One day, Lewis reported, McNeal's horse "took the allarm and turning short threw him immediately under the bear." McNeal stunned the bear by hitting it on its head with his gun, giving him time to scramble up a tree.

July 11, 1806 (Day 789)

It took just nine days to get to the Great Falls — almost six weeks and 400 miles (644 km) less than it had taken the previous summer. The Indian shortcuts certainly came in handy! The men made Mandan-style bullboats (pages 98–99) and paddled across the Missouri above Great Falls to their old camp on White Bear Islands, where supplies were hidden.

Deadly Encounter

July 26, 1806 (Day 804)

While Gass and five privates stayed to portage the supplies around the falls, Lewis and three others rode off to explore the Marias (page 71). On July 26, they met up with eight Blackfeet warriors. At first the encounter was friendly and Lewis suggested they camp together. The Indians made a shelter with willow branches and buffalo skins. With Drouillard signing, Lewis talked about Americans establishing peace and trade with other Indian tribes. It couldn't have been what the Blackfeet wanted to hear. It meant their enemies would soon be getting guns and whites would compete with them for trade.

That may have been why the Indians tried to steal the explorers' rifles and horses at dawn the next day. The Field brothers dashed after the Indian who took their rifles and wrestled him to the ground. In the scuffle, Reuben Field stabbed him. Lewis was forced to shoot another Indian who threatened him with a gun. On July 27, both Blackfeet died. Lewis and his men rode hard all day and night to get back to the Missouri.

PORTRAIT BY KARL BODMER, *MEHKSKEME-SUKAHS, BLACKFOOT CHIEF*

Clark's Route

Clark's party included 20 men, Sacagawea and Pomp (now a year and a half old), and 50 horses. They followed a shortcut across the Continental Divide the Salish (page 82) had told them about the year before (now called Bozeman Pass). When they entered a level plain, reported Clark, the "Indian trail Scattered in Such a manner that we Could not pursue it." Fortunately, Sacagawea knew the way to Camp Fortunate on the Beaverhead River, where they recovered the canoes and supplies they had hidden.

Clark's party, some in the canoes on the Beaverhead and Jefferson rivers, some on horseback, then headed northeast to Three Forks. The trip took 14 fewer days than the way west had. Ordway took a few men down the Missouri to White Bear Islands to help Gass with the portage. Clark's party went overland to the Yellowstone River, reaching it near what's now Livingston, Montana. Once again, Clark reported, Sacagawea pointed the way through "a gap in the mountains" to "an old buffalow road."

At the Yellowstone, they found trees large enough to make two long, narrow canoes, which they lashed together to make a raft. On the night of July 20, while everyone slept, Indians stole 24 of their horses. As Sergeant Pryor and three privates drove the remaining horses on shore, Clark and the others took the raft down the Yellowstone to the Missouri. Along one stretch Clark noted that "grasshoppers have distroyed every Sprig of Grass for maney miles." Once they had to stop for more than an hour to let a huge "gangue [gang] of Buffalow" swim across the river. Twice grizzly bears, probably smelling the buffalo meat on board, plunged into the river and chased the raft!

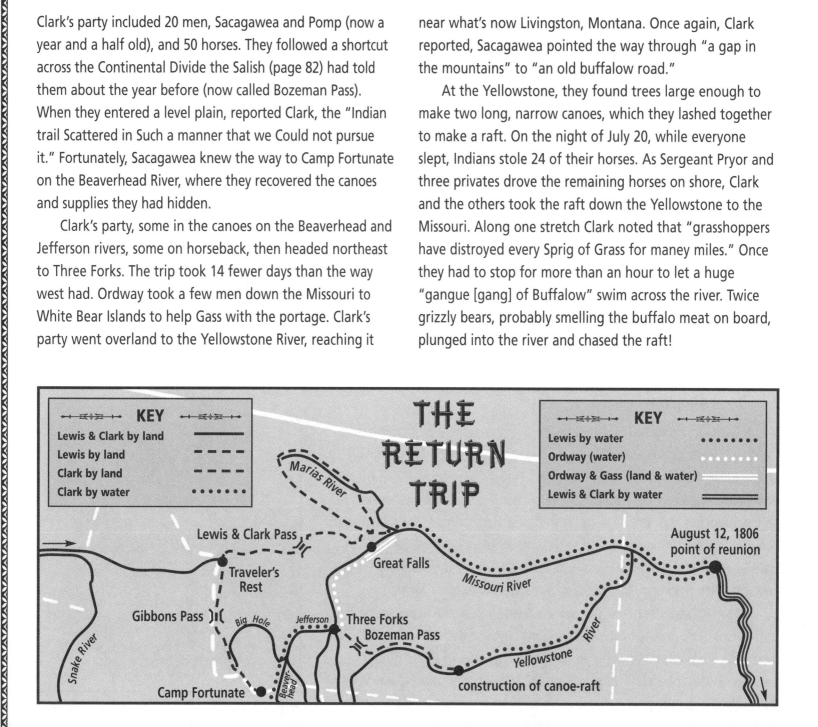

KEY
Lewis & Clark by land ——————
Lewis by land — — — —
Clark by land – – – –
Clark by water • • • • • •

KEY
Lewis by water • • • • • • •
Ordway (water) ∘ ∘ ∘ ∘ ∘ ∘ ∘
Ordway & Gass (land & water) ——————
Lewis & Clark by water ══════

THE RETURN TRIP

Marias River

Lewis & Clark Pass

Great Falls

August 12, 1806 point of reunion

Traveler's Rest

Missouri River

Gibbons Pass

Big Hole

Jefferson

Three Forks

Bozeman Pass

Snake River

Camp Fortunate

Beaverhead

Yellowstone River

construction of canoe-raft

More Horses Stolen!

The plan was for Sergeant Pryor and the privates to drive the remaining horses back to the Mandans as gifts. But on the second night, Crow Indians stole them. Carrying heavy backpacks, the men marched to the river. There, Shannon made two bullboats. The four men climbed aboard and followed Clark down the Yellowstone. They met his party on the Missouri on August 8.

Worth the Risk?

The most important goal of the expedition at this time was to get back to St. Louis safely with all the important documents, maps, and specimens. Splitting the Corps into smaller groups put them all in danger. After all they were traveling through an area where war parties and hunters from Crow, Blackfeet, and Hidatsa villages roamed. The captains obviously wanted to explore as much as possible, but was that a good enough reason to risk the expedition? Probably not. It's likely that Lewis and Clark were overconfident in their own and their men's ability to handle Indians. It gave them some frightening moments and cost two Blackfeet their lives (page 95).

Lewis Shot!

August 12, 1806 (Day 821)

On August 12, Lewis's party rejoined Clark's on the Missouri. Lewis was lying face down in the white pirogue. The day before, he had been shot by one-eyed Cruzatte who mistook him for the elk they were hunting! When Clark saw Lewis, he was "alarmed" and treated the wound. Where was Lewis shot? In his behind! Fortunately, the bullet didn't hit a bone or sever an artery. The wound was so painful, however, that Lewis stopped writing in his journal — but not before describing a new kind of cherry. It was his last journal entry.

BUILD A BULLBOAT

The Mandans and Hidatsas crossed the Missouri River in bullboats, half moon–shaped boats made by stretching a single buffalo hide over a frame of willow branches. Hunters tied several boats together to carry their cargo of meat and hides. Lewis, Shannon, and others learned how to make them at Fort Mandan (page 53) — they might not have realized they would come in so handy!

Supplies

➤ Large brown paper bag
➤ Large mixing bowl
➤ Old newspaper
➤ Paper towels
➤ Poster board
➤ Scissors
➤ Tape
➤ Tape measure
➤ All-purpose, nontoxic sealer
➤ Foam brush

To prepare the buffalo hide:

Tear off a piece of brown paper large enough to wrap around the bowl. Soak the paper in water. Squeeze (don't wring) it out and spread it flat on the newspaper. Blot with paper towels.

To make the frame:

❶ Cut a long strip of poster board, about ½" (1 cm) wide. Tape it into a circle that fits around the rim of the large bowl. This circle will become the rim of the boat's frame.

❷ Turn the bowl upside down and measure the distance over it from one side to the other. Add 6" (15 cm) to that length. Cut eight strips of poster board that length and about ½" (1 cm) wide.

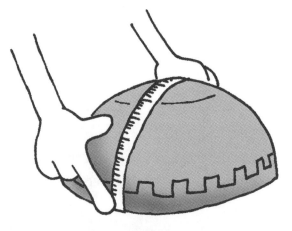

❸ Slip the poster-board circle over the upside-down bowl so it rests on the table. Slip one end of a strip inside the circle, bend it up, and tape it in place.

Lay the other end over the bowl and tape the end to the circle in the same way.

Repeat with all the strips until you have what looks like a basket frame. Tape the strips together where they crisscross at the bottom (don't tape the strips to the bowl).

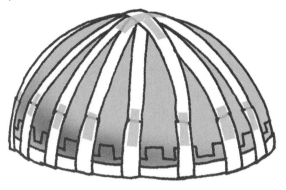

To cover the boat:

❶ When your "buffalo hide" (the brown paper) is still slightly damp and flexible, lay it flat on a table and place the frame in the center. Mark four points around the rim of your frame (the circle) to divide it into quarters.

❷ Bring an edge of the buffalo hide up and over the rim at one of the marks so there's at least an inch (2.5 cm) inside the rim. Tape it down. Do the same at the mark on the opposite side of the rim.

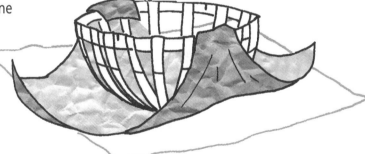

Cut the hide if it hangs over too much. Repeat the process at the other two marks so the hide is attached at these four points.

❸ In between where the hide is attached, it will drape in big folds. Working one section at a time, crease the excess, fold it over the rim and tape down. Continue until the hide is completely wrapped around the frame. Tape the hide all around the inside of the rim. If it's still damp, let dry.

❹ To waterproof your bullboat, coat it with the sealer. After it dries, look it over. Would you trust it to carry precious cargo across a river? A creek? How about the bathtub? Test it and find out!

Note: Please ask an adult for permission to fill the bathtub and to supervise if infants and toddlers are nearby.

Breakdown of Peace

August 15, 1806 (Day 824)

By August 15, the Corps was back among the Mandans. The news was bad. All the promises for peace between the warring Indian nations had been broken. Sioux warriors had raided the Mandans, the Mandans and Arikaras had fought, and the Hidatsas had attacked the Shoshones. With Lewis injured, Clark alone had to try to persuade a Mandan leader to come with the expedition and meet President Jefferson. Finally, Sheheke Shoat agreed, if he could bring his wife and son.

Then Clark paid Charbonneau $500, said good-bye to Sacagawea, and offered to adopt Pomp. He loved "the little dancing boy" and promised to "educate him and treat him as my own child." The baby's parents declined for the time being. Then, the Corps and their Indian friends headed downriver to St. Louis.

O! The Joy! Cow in View!

September 23, 1806 (Day 863: The End of the Expedition)

The expedition passed the Teton Sioux with little trouble and visited the grave of Charles Floyd (page 50). Soon they were meeting fur traders on the river, including an old Army friend of Lewis's. He, according to Clark, "was Somewhat astonished to See us" and informed them that "we had been long Since given [up] by the people of the US."

Then a really incredible sight! "We Saw Some cows on the bank which ... Caused a Shout to be raised for joy," Clark wrote. To men anxious to be home, a cow for once seemed as exciting as the Pacific Ocean. Each time they passed a village, the men shot their guns in salute and people along the banks cheered in disbelief at the Corps' survival.

They pulled into St. Louis at noon on September 23, nearly two and a half years after they had departed. Lewis immediately wrote a long letter to Jefferson: "It is with pleasure that I announce to you the safe arrival of myself and party ... with our papers and baggage." Clark took

Wow! A cow!

Sheheke Shoat and his family shopping for calico shirts, fancy handkerchiefs, and American clothes. That night Lewis and Clark stayed with their friends, the Chouteaus. The men, Ordway wrote, were looking forward to receiving their pay and returning home "to See our parents once more as we have been So long from them." St. Louis celebrated with a grand dinner and a ball.

A TRUE VOYAGE OF DISCOVERY

President Jefferson received the news of the Corps' safe return to St. Louis with "unspeakable joy." He wrote Lewis that his long absence "had begun to be felt awfully" and to tell Sheheke Shoat that "I have already opened my arms to receive him." Later, Jefferson wrote that "never did a similar event excite more joy through the United States." And so it must have seemed to Lewis, Clark, and Sheheke Shoat as they traveled east. Towns held balls in their honor. Newspaper headlines described their adventures. It took 31 days for Lewis's letter to get to Jefferson. It took Lewis more than three months to travel from St. Louis to Washington!

Imagine the welcome Lewis received from the president. Would Jefferson have a bear hug for this young man he was so fond of? A formal handshake? We don't know. With all the writing these men did, they didn't write about that moment. We do know Jefferson spread the latest maps on the floor and examined them closely, and urged Lewis to publish his journals as soon as possible. The president must have been thrilled to see that the expedition had fulfilled most of his goals.

The detailed maps, the scientific descriptions of 122 animals and 178 plants, and the studies of many diverse Indian nations were exactly what Jefferson had wanted. The lack of an easy waterway across the continent and the failed attempts at peacemaking among tribes were probably disappointing. Other discoveries would change Jefferson's vision of the West. Sure, there were areas of swamps as well as dry, barren land, but the Great Plains were a huge, fertile area alive with game and dotted with Indian villages. The Columbia River's shores were rich with Indian life. And while some Indian tribes were indeed hostile and violent — much more to each other than to whites — the expedition's journals made it clear that each American Indian nation had its own distinct culture just as all nations do.

Whatever Happened to ...

After the expedition was over, the close-knit members of the Corps and the people they met went their separate ways.

Meriwether Lewis was made governor of the Louisiana Territory in 1807, but politics and St. Louis didn't suit his personality. Unable to keep up with political demands, find a wife, or keep out of debt, he also couldn't organize his journals

for publication. William Clark remained a true friend, but even he couldn't help. Feeling like a failure, Lewis began drinking too much and sank into depression. On his way to Washington in October 1809, he committed suicide. He was only 35. Jefferson later wrote that his act "deprived his country of one of her most valued citizens."

After Lewis's death, Clark convinced a young Philadelphia lawyer named Nicholas Biddle to edit the journals into a book. Corps member George Shannon (page 103) helped. But Biddle's 1814 edition left out much of the science, something that Lewis had planned to devote an entire volume to. That meant that Lewis and Clark were not given full credit for their many descriptions of new plants and animals. It took another 90 years for the complete journals to be edited.

William Clark married 16-year-old Julia Hancock and moved to St. Louis when Jefferson appointed him Superintendent of Indian Affairs of the Louisiana Territory. Later he was governor of the Missouri Territory. The Clarks named their oldest son Meriwether after his father's "equal partner." After Julia died, Clark remarried. Altogether he fathered seven children, raised three step-children, and was guardian to Pomp and a second child of Sacagawea's.

Clark's jobs put him in charge of 100,000 Indians living on the Missouri and upper Mississippi rivers. As he looked out for American interests in treaties with tribes, he also tried to give the Indians as fair a deal as possible. He believed Indians should be treated with "justice and humanity." Clark remained a friend of the Indians until his death in 1838. His gravestone reads: "His life is written in the history of his country."

York went from being essentially a free man who shouldered his share of duties and hardships on the journey, back to being a slave. Even though he had worked as hard as anyone else, he was not paid for his service or given a grant of land, as the other men were. In 1808, York asked Clark for his freedom so he could return to Kentucky where his wife was owned by another man. Clark angrily refused and began to treat York poorly. Finally, about eight years later, Clark freed York and set him up in a freight wagon business, which failed. York reportedly died of cholera sometime before 1832.

Sacagawea and **Toussaint Charbonneau** remained with the Hidatsa. When **Pomp** (Jean Baptiste) was 4, the family moved to St. Louis. Two years later, his parents returned to Indian country, but left Pomp with Clark, who became his guardian. In December 1812, in a fort in South Dakota, Sacagawea gave birth to a girl, Lizette. Shortly after, Sacagawea died from a fever, and Clark took in Lizette, who died as a baby. Toussaint Charbonneau continued as an interpreter until he died of old age.

POMP

Jean Baptiste was educated and spent time in Europe as a young man. He could speak English, Hidatsa and Shoshone, German, French, and Italian, and knew Latin and Greek. When he returned to the United States, he became a trapper in the mountains of present-day Idaho and Utah, serving as a guide and interpreter for Army officers and explorers. At age 61 on a wagon train to Montana to look for gold, Jean Baptiste died of pneumonia.

Patrick Gass published his journal in 1807, lost his left eye in the War of 1812 (a war between the U.S. and Britain), and eventually settled in West Virginia. At 60, he married a woman some 40 years younger and had seven children. He died in 1870, two months before his 99th birthday, the last surviving member of the Corps. In his lifetime, the United States was born, grew from 13 to 38 states, and barely survived the Civil War. He saw steamboats replace keelboats and railroads replace wagon trains.

John Ordway visited his parents in New Hampshire before getting married and moving to Missouri. There he farmed his 320 acres (128 hectares) until he died in 1817. He sold his journals to Lewis and Clark for $300 in 1807.

John Colter set off from the Mandan villages to become a trapper. He was the first non-Indian to see the geysers in what became Yellowstone National Park in Wyoming and supplied details to Clark, who used them to update his map. In 1810, Colter and his trapping partner and co-member

of the Corps, **John Potts**, were captured by Blackfeet. Potts was killed, but Colter escaped by running naked across hundreds of miles (km). He married an Indian woman, settled near Daniel Boone in Missouri, and died in 1813.

George Drouillard was killed in 1810 by Blackfeet warriors while trapping near Three Forks.

In 1807, **Nathaniel Pryor** led a small expedition that included **George Shannon** to escort **Sheheke Shoat** home. The Arikaras, angry because their own chief had gotten sick and died while on a visit to Washington, attacked their boat. Shannon was shot and lost a leg. He married, became a lawyer, and entered politics in Missouri. Pryor left the Army in 1814 after his first wife died. He became an Indian trader and married an Osage woman. He died in 1831.

Today, the vast **prairie** that Lewis and Clark found is almost gone. So are the 50 million buffalo that roamed it. There are only 20 small areas of prairie left, and the wild buffalo number about 20,000. In the Northern Rockies and the Pacific Northwest, much of the forests the expedition passed through have been felled by logging, and the grizzly population has dropped from 100,000 to fewer than 1,000.

The **American Indians** that Lewis and Clark met faced devastation in the decades that followed. Hidatsa warriors killed Sacagawea's brother, **Cameahwait**. Traders burned **Coboway's Clatsop** village. A **Teton Sioux** attack in 1834 destroyed two Hidatsa villages. Three years later, a smallpox epidemic killed nine out of ten **Mandans**. Since 1885, the Mandans, **Hidatsas**, and **Arikaras** have lived together on the Fort Berthold Reservation in North Dakota. Today they are known as the Three Affiliated Tribes.
In 1876, after decades of fighting with settlers and the U.S. Army, the Teton Sioux helped defeat General George Armstrong Custer at the Battle of Little Bighorn (near the Little Bighorn River in Montana); by the next spring they were on reservations. The next year, some of the **Nez Perce** tried to escape to Canada to avoid going on a reservation. The Army tracked them down. After many battles, some of the tribe that saved the starving Corps surrendered; others escaped north over the border.

Contradictions

On the expedition, York worked, ate, and slept side by side with white men. He carried a rifle and was allowed to vote. The captains trusted him on hunting and trading trips. The rest of the men accepted him as an equal. Yet Clark kept him as a slave upon their return. Jefferson and Lewis probably saw nothing wrong with that. These three great men all owned slaves. And yet Jefferson wrote that slavery turned owners into tyrants and degraded the owned, and hoped slavery would be abolished one day. It was one of the great contradictions in his life.

The attitude of Jefferson and the Corps members toward Indians was also complicated. The expedition made them see Indians as separate nations and, more important, as individuals. Lewis didn't live long enough to see what happened to the Indians as a result of American expansion into the West. Clark did what he could to help them as long as he lived. Jefferson actually set policies that eventually took their land, culture, and often their lives away from them.

Still a Bargain?

Remember the $2,500 that President Jefferson told Congress the expedition would cost (page 7)? Well, Lewis spent more than that before he even left Pittsburgh! Then, in St. Louis, he spent another $15,000 on supplies and salaries for the boatmen. At the end of the expedition, Lewis's tally came to $38,722.25, more than 15 times the original estimate. Add in the price of the land that each of the men received as a reward, and the total topped $136,000. In today's dollars, that's more than $120,000,000 (one hundred and twenty million dollars)! Considering that it cost about *25 billion* dollars to send a crew of men to the moon, Lewis and Clark's expedition was still quite a bargain!

WELL GENTLEMEN, iT SEEMS THAT WE'VE GONE A TEENY-TiNY BiT OVER BUDGET, HEH, HEH.

A Voyage of Discovery and Change

The Lewis and Clark expedition was a heroic undertaking led by and carried out by heroic men. Heroes — great people — are not perfect people, but they have great thoughts and accomplish great deeds. The expedition combined incredible planning, great coaching, terrific teamwork, creative moves, and a little bit of luck, as well as lots of invaluable help from many different Indian tribes. It filled in the blank, empty area on old maps with a West that was dynamic and alive. Not finding an all-water route didn't matter in the end. Later, other explorers found easier passes over the Continental Divide and the Rockies, like trapper Jedediah Smith who found Wyoming's South Pass in 1824.

The West that Lewis and Clark had discovered fired up the imagination of the young country. Businessmen created fur-trading empires, scientists studied new animals and plants, and explorers mapped the new geography. In the decades to come, the U.S. acquired the Oregon Country and California. Hundreds of thousands of Americans and people from distant lands poured into the West across South Pass on the Oregon Trail. The vast plains were settled in just a few generations, and by 1869, the huge nation was linked coast to coast by telegraph and transcontinental railroad. All these changes, started by Lewis and Clark, created the strong continental nation Thomas Jefferson had envisioned.

RESOURCES

January 2003 marks the beginning of a three-year American celebration of the bicentennial (200-year anniversary) of the Louisiana Purchase and the Lewis & Clark expedition. Join in celebrating the grand adventure with these great resources.

Books to Read

Blumberg, Rhoda. *The Incredible Journey of Lewis & Clark.* Beach Tree Books, 1995.

Bruchac, Joseph. *Sacajawea: The Story of Bird Woman and the Lewis and Clark Expedition.* Scholastic Paperbacks, 2001.

Cavan, Seamus. *Lewis and Clark and the Route to the Pacific.* Chelsea House Publishers, 1991.

Gunderson, Mary. *Cooking on the Lewis and Clark Expedition.* Blue Earth Books, 2000.

Karwoski, Gail Langer. *Seaman: The Dog Who Explored the West with Lewis & Clark.* Peachtree Publishers, 1999.

Lewis and Clark: Explorers of the American West. Steven Kroll, Holiday House, 1996.

Morley, Jacqueline. *Across America: The Story of Lewis & Clark.* Franklin Watts, 1998.

Roop, Peter and Connie. *Off the Map: The Journals of Lewis and Clark.* Walker & Company, 1998.

St. George, Judith. *Sacagawea.* Putnam Publishing Group, 1997.

Schanzer, Rosalyn. *How We Crossed the West: The Adventures of Lewis & Clark.* National Geographic Society, 1997.

Websites to Explore

Visit **www.williamsonbooks.com** for a listing of websites and exhibitions on the Lewis & Clark expedition.

To order Mandan corn seeds (p. 77):

Mandan Red corn
Seeds of Change
P.O. Box 15700
Santa Fe, NM 87506
(888) 762-7333
www.seedsofchange.com

Mandan Bride corn
Abundant Life Seed Foundation
P.O. Box 772
Port Townsend, WA 98368
(360) 385-5660
www.abundantlifeseed.org

Videos & Movies to Enjoy

Lewis & Clark: Great Journey West, produced by Jeff T. Miller and Lisa Truitt, 45 minutes, National Geographic Society, 2002, IMAX (large format) film, videocassette, and DVD

Lewis & Clark: The Journey of the Corps of Discovery, a film by Ken Burns, Florentine Films and WETA-TV, produced by Ken Burns and Dayton Duncan, 4 hours, PBS Home Video, 1997, videocassette and DVD

Free Teacher's Guide!

If you are a schoolteacher or are homeschooling your family, please visit our website <**www.williamsonbooks.com**> and click on "For Teachers, Parents, & Caregivers" to download a FREE Teacher's Guide with additional classroom ideas, activities, and projects.

From the author

The idea for this book came to me as I read Stephen E. Ambrose's *Undaunted Courage: Meriwether Lewis, Thomas Jefferson, and the Opening of the American West* (Simon & Schuster, 1996). James P. Ronda's *Lewis and Clark Among the Indians* (University of Nebraska Press, 1984) and *Finding the West: Explorations with Lewis and Clark* (University of New Mexico Press, 2001) helped round out my perspective on both the crucial role American Indians played in the expedition and early nineteenth-century fascination with the West.

The documentary film *Lewis & Clark: The Journey of the Corps of Discovery* by Ken Burns and Dayton Duncan (PBS Home Video, 1997), and its companion book, gave me a sense of traveling with the Corps, as did Sam Abell's photography in *Lewis & Clark: Voyage of Discovery* (Ambrose, National Geographic Society, 1998) and Thomas Schmidt's *The Lewis & Clark Trail* (National Geographic Society, 1998), a must-have guidebook for anyone traveling the trail today.

Finally, no book on Lewis and Clark can be written without turning to the words of the "writingest explorers" themselves. All quotations in this book are from *Letters of the Lewis and Clark Expedition with Related Documents 1783–1854*, edited by Donald Jackson (University of Illinois Press, 1978), and *The Journals of the Lewis & Clark Expedition,* edited by Gary E. Moulton (University of Nebraska Press, 1986–2001). Gunther Barth's *The Lewis and Clark Expedition: Selections from the Journals Arranged by Topic* (Bedford/St. Martin's, 1998) and Landon Y. Jones's *The Essential Lewis and Clark* (The Ecco Press, 2000) helped guide me through 11 of Moulton's volumes.

Be a Williamson *You Can Do It!*™ Winner!

Send us your project photos & writings to enter!

NOW you can see selected projects from readers just like you posted on our website! And one project per month will be named a *You Can Do It!*™ Winner! The winning child, family, or group will receive a gift certificate for Williamson Books. If your project is posted on our website, you will receive an official Certificate for Great Work!

How to enter:
- Send us a photo or e-mail us a PDF or JPEG file of your project. If you have written entries, please e-mail or send them to us.
- Attach your name and age to all entries.
- If your class sends an entry or your whole family participates, let us know that, too! The more, the merrier!
- Check out our website to see if your entry gets posted.
- Be sure to send us your address so we can notify you if you win!

E-mail entries to:
winner@williamsonbooks.com
or mail to:
Winner
Williamson Books
P.O. Box 185
Charlotte, Vermont 05445

WIN a gift certificate! New winner every month!

Notice: We are not responsible for materials sent. Do not send us the whole project — just the photos — which will not be returned. Do not send us the only copy of something you write or draw, because we cannot return it. If posted, the project photo or written work will show your first name, last initial, your state or country, and your age. We will notify you only if you win.

Visit our website to see if your project is posted and to see if you are a Williamson Winner: **www.williamsonbooks.com**.

Entries must be from children aged 14 and younger. Judging will be done by a group of assorted, changing people who by nature will have different preferences. Originality, problem-solving ability, creativity, sensitivity to others, and skill in presentation will be judged. Williamson Publishing acknowledges that judging is subjective and will not be held accountable for the judges' decisions. All those who don't win are eligible to enter multiple times, using a different project each time. One gift certificate per project no matter how many creators! No last names or addresses of winners of posted work will be shown on our website — ever! Not open to families of our authors or our staff, or those who have won a prize in the last year.

INDEX

MORE GOOD BOOKS FROM WILLIAMSON PUBLISHING

Kaleidoscope Kids® books for ages 7 to 14, are 96 pages, fully illustrated, 10 x 10, $12.95 US/$19.95 CAN.

Also by Carol A. Johmann:

ForeWord Magazine Book of the Year Finalist
SKYSCRAPERS!
Super Structures to Design & Build

Benjamin Franklin Silver Award
GOING WEST!
Journey on a Wagon Train to Settle a Frontier Town
by Carol A. Johmann and Elizabeth J. Rieth

Parents' Choice Recommended
BRIDGES!
Amazing Structures to Design, Build & Test
by Carol A. Johmann and Elizabeth J. Rieth

ANCIENT ROME!
Exploring the Culture, People & Ideas of This Powerful Empire
by Avery Hart and Sandra Gallagher

Children's Book Council Notable Book
WHO *REALLY* DISCOVERED AMERICA?
Unraveling the Mystery & Solving the Puzzle
by Avery Hart

American Bookseller Pick of the Lists
¡MEXICO!
40 Activities to Experience Mexico Past and Present
by Susan Milord

Children's Book Council Notable Book
American Bookseller Pick of the Lists
KNIGHTS & CASTLES
50 Hands-On Activities to Experience the Middle Ages
by Avery Hart and Paul Mantell

THE BEAST IN YOU!
Activities & Questions to Explore Evolution
by Marc McCutcheon

American Bookseller Pick of the Lists
Parent's Guide Children's Media Award
ANCIENT GREECE!
40 Hands-On Activities to Experience This Wondrous Age
by Avery Hart and Paul Mantell

Children's Book Council Notable Book
Dr. Toy 10 Best Educational Products
PYRAMIDS!
50 Hands-On Activities to Experience Ancient Egypt
by Avery Hart and Paul Mantell

Teachers' Choice Award
GEOLOGY ROCKS!
50 Hands-On Activities to Explore the Earth
by Cindy Blobaum

Enter our contest!
To learn more, see page 108. To learn more about specific books, visit our website at:
www.williamsonbooks.com

To order books:

You'll find Williamson books wherever high-quality children's books are sold. To order directly from Williamson Publishing,

go to our secure website: **www.williamsonbooks.com**

call toll-free with credit cards: **1-800-234-8791**

We accept Visa and MasterCard (please include the number and expiration date). Or, send a check with your order to:

Williamson Publishing
P.O. Box 185
Charlotte, Vermont 05445

For a free catalog: mail, phone, or e-mail

info@williamsonbooks.com

Please add **$4.00** for postage for one book plus **$1.00** for each additional book. Satisfaction is guaranteed or full refund without questions or quibbles.